Breaking Free

*Overcoming Depression Through
Biblical Principles*

Randall Rittenberry

Emphasis within scripture quotations is the author's own.

Breaking Free
Overcoming Depression Through Biblical Principles

ISBN: **979-8-9887417-1-8**

Printed in the United States of America

Copyright © 2023 by Randall Rittenberry

Chapter Design: Freepik

Compass Publishing USA

Table of Contents

Chapter 1
Are You Ready?

————•◇◇•————

As we begin our journey, let's get something out of the way: depression is a prison. It binds the individual emotionally, mentally, and physically. It affects every aspect of life: relationships, ambitions, jobs, etc. Personally, I suffered from depression from a young age until I was thirty years old. I can remember having thoughts of inadequacy as early as four years old. I understand what it is like to live in that prison. But I also know how to be free from that prison as well. There are principles that I have learned and applied from God's word that not only set me free, but also keep me free. My goal is to share these principles with you in this book.

These principles will work for anyone. Biblical principles are eternal and exhaustive, which means they are absolute when applied. When you are trapped in depression, it seems as if no one understands. It seems like you are all alone. Trust me; that is not true. The emotions of depression are not unique to any one person. 1 Corinthians 10:13 says, *"The temptations in your life are no different from what others experience..."* (NLT). satan tells you these things to isolate you and keep you from seeking the counsel of God. If he can keep you in that prison, he can rob you of everything God intends for your life, including your purpose. If you are ready, then the principles here can set you free from depression.

Embracing Truth

The only way to be free from anything is to start at the beginning: the truth! If you are truly ready to walk out of depression, then you must be ready to embrace truth as presented in God's word. In John 8:32, Jesus said, *"And you shall know the truth, and the truth shall make you free."* It is a saying we have all heard and most likely used at some point in our life, at least the last part of the saying anyway. But what is often missed is the preceding verse, John 8:31 *"Then said Jesus to those Jews which believed on him, If you continue in my word, then are you my disciples indeed…"* It is not the truth that sets you free; it is **knowing and continuing in** the truth that brings freedom.

Jesus is saying in these two verses that the only way to know the truth is to continue in His word. If we are unwilling to consider God's word as the standard of truth, then we will never be free from whatever binds us, including depression. This is the foundational principle: God's word is truth, and I will follow the principles set within His word. We must be willing to acknowledge the truth, no matter how difficult it may seem. There may be times when the truth is uncomfortable. There may be times when the truth hurts. As the old saying goes, "The truth may set you free, but first, it will make you mad." As my mentor, Dr. Jim Richards, points out, "The truth that sets you free has the potential to be the thing that offends you the most."

One of the first principles I learned in overcoming my depression is this: only you can change yourself. Now, when I say that only you can change yourself, I do not mean that God cannot help or does not play a part. Of course, He does. It is His word and His principles, after all. What I mean is that we cannot place the responsibility of change onto any external source or person. One of the thoughts I consistently had was that if a certain person would acknowledge their part in my hurt, then change would come. I put the burden of freedom onto a scenario that might never happen. I put my hope into that scenario and that person.

Other people are not our problem. Circumstances are not our problem. They become a problem when we place our hope on them. Many times, depression forms because situations do not turn out as we expect. People do not respond the way we think they will or should. The sooner we remove our selfish expectations from external sources, the quicker we get to freedom. When we place our hope and expectations on others or even circumstances, it is called 'co-dependency.' In simplest terms, it means that we are clinging to something other than God to fulfill our needs.

Life is fluid and ever-changing; to place our hope in something that is in a constant state of change is unhealthy and dangerous. That is why Paul said, *"Not that I speak in respect of want: for I have learned, in whatsoever state I am, therewith to be content."* (Phil. 4:11) Likewise, it is unhealthy and dangerous to place our hope on other people. God did not design us to be the root source of happiness for anyone else. We contribute to others' happiness and well-being, but no person can be what only God can be for us. The first step out of prison towards freedom is taking responsibility for our own lives.

Since the word of God is our standard for truth, we must look there to get on the right path to victory. *"Thy word is a lamp unto my feet, and a light unto my path."* (Psalm 119:105) We are presented with two ways of life in everything: the way of the kingdom of God and the way of the world system. The world system will provide treatment; the kingdom of God will provide freedom. The world system will tell you that you are depressed because you are not expressing yourself but that you are suppressing yourself; the kingdom of God says to look to Jesus, not yourself. The world system will tell you to look externally for blame; the kingdom of God says to examine your own heart.

The world system will tell you medication is the only way you can live a functional life through depression; the kingdom of God says you do not have to be a slave to anything. Now, let me say this: I am NOT saying that medication is wrong. I am NOT saying it is not beneficial and, at times, necessary. Thank God for medicine! What I AM saying, though, is that medication is a means to an end; it is not the end itself. If we are not careful, we will trade one prison for another. We will look at medication in another chapter. My point is that freedom can only come through one system of life: the kingdom of God!

Secondary Gains

If you are truly ready to travel the road ahead, you must lay aside what is known as 'secondary gains.' A secondary gain is any benefit we receive or perceive that we receive from behavior, habits, hobbies, relationships, etc. The term is used primarily in the medical and psychological fields. It describes positive advantages obtained incidentally through illness. People can receive treatment for a basic, curable illness but never become well if they have attached a secondary gain to that illness. I have seen people refuse treatment and even prayer because they have a financial incentive to stay where they are. It sounds far-fetched, but there is a Biblical premise to this notion.

In the Gospel of John, Chapter Five, we see the account of the man with an infirmity at the pool of Bethesda. People with illnesses would wait at this pool, and when an angel would 'trouble' the water, the first one into the pool would be healed. When Jesus saw this man, the first thing He asked him was, *"Will you be made whole?"* The man's first response was an excuse: *"I have no one to put me into the pool, and others beat me to it."* In the end of the account, the man was healed.

I used to read this and wonder why Jesus would ask such a question. My reasoning was that anyone would want to be healed, especially of an illness they had carried for thirty-eight years and had debilitated them. What we later find in the account is Jesus instructing the man not to sin anymore so that a worse thing does not come upon him. This reveals that the man had used his illness to avoid responsibility. It was a 'secondary gain' for him. He reasoned that as long as he was ill, he would never have to deal with his issues. After Jesus spoke to him about no longer sinning, the man told the Jewish leaders that Jesus had healed him on the Sabbath. He became offended at Jesus for removing his excuse. In his offense, he 'ratted out' Jesus, the one who brought him healing. This also points to the man having a 'secondary gain.' Notice that this man was healed; his excuse was removed. However, the question Jesus asked him was, *"Do you want to be made* **whole?***".*

There is a difference between being healed and being made whole. When a sickness or infirmity has a secondary gain attached to it, then when healing comes it is only temporary unless that issue is confronted and resolved. Likewise, if negative heart issues develop through sickness or infirmity, then those issues must be confronted and resolved so wholeness can happen. In Mark 10:46-52, we see the account of blind Bartimaeus. He was a beggar on the highway outside of Jericho. He heard Jesus was passing his way and began to cry out for Jesus to heal him. When Jesus called to him, verse 50 records that Bartimaeus *"casting away his garment, rose, and came to Jesus."* The garment that he cast away was a beggar's garment. It was his legal right under Roman law that allowed him to beg for money due to his blindness. Bartimaeus cast off his secondary gain. This was Jesus' response in verses 51 and 52: *"What wilt thou that I should do unto thee? The blind man said unto him, Lord, that I might receive my sight. And Jesus said unto him, Go thy way; thy faith hath made thee* **whole***. And immediately he received his sight, and followed Jesus in the way."*

If you genuinely want to be free from depression, you must let go of everything that keeps you attached to it. This includes financial benefits, sympathy, avoiding responsibility, habits, and even the emotions that have become familiar due to depression. Emotions can be like drugs and can have the same chemical effect on your body that a drug would produce. We get used to that chemical effect, creating an addiction; this is true for both negative and positive emotions. This is why it can be challenging to let go and why people may stay in bad situations, incomprehensible to others. The crucial question you must ask yourself is, "Are those things worth my freedom?"

Having counseled numerous people over the years, I've witnessed individuals engaging in destructive behaviors and forming harmful habits. I've seen people hurt others and feel remorse, and yet continue those actions. As the saying goes, "hurting people hurt people." Why would anyone choose to stay in such a situation? They are addicted, not to a substance but to their emotions. More precisely, they are addicted to the chemical rush those emotions create. Changing oneself requires a personal choice to break those secondary gains, habits, and emotional attachments. It entails making the choice to let God's word guide you through the process. In the upcoming chapters, we will explore the causes and effects of depression and apply Biblical principles that lead to transformation.

Are you ready?
Will you be made whole?

Chapter 2
Basic Information

———•◇◇◇•———

Depression has been scientifically proven to impact both the brain and the body, influencing overall health and quality of life. The repercussions on the brain and body may extend to conditions such as epilepsy, migraines, stroke, Parkinson's disease, and dementia.[1] Additionally, depression can contribute to symptoms like fatigue, chronic pain, gastrointestinal issues, and heart disease.[2] As we progress throughout this chapter, we will delve into the various ways in which depression affects our brain and body. Please pay attention to the superscript numbers, which correspond to the bibliography at the end of the book. The bibliography includes notes and links for further research.

Chemical Imbalance

We must mention the subject of chemical imbalance when addressing depression. Conventional science has presented chemical imbalance as the cause of depression. Chemical imbalance is defined as either too much or too little of chemicals, called neurotransmitters, between nerve cells in the brain. Many medications are prescribed to prevent chemical imbalance. In 1996, my wife and I were discussing a family member who had been diagnosed with chemical imbalance. This family member received medication to offset the imbalance. Since I had struggled with depression from an early age, I began to wonder if I needed medication as well. As I prayed about it, I heard the Holy

Spirit tell me that chemical imbalance did not cause depression; the depression caused the chemical imbalance.

Several studies since then now show the distinct possibility that chemical imbalance is not the cause of depression; rather, it is a symptom. Medications that are given to help with chemical imbalance do not alleviate depression. They simply elevate mood and lessen the effect of depression.[3] Medications can help bring relief, but we must realize they are only treating a symptom and not the root cause. As I said before, they may be needed, but if the root cause is not dealt with, then they become a band-aid at best and a co-dependent prison at worst. In the story, I related what the Holy Spirit revealed to me about chemical imbalance; it was also revealed to me what the root cause was. We will begin to address that root cause in the next chapter.

Effects on the Brain

Depression, especially when untreated, can alter the brain. The hippocampus, which regulates learning and memory, releases a hormone called cortisol during times of stress and duress. This can lead to interruptions in learning and memory problems. The same release of cortisol also affects the amygdala, the part of the brain that controls emotional behavior and motivation. That is why prolonged bouts of depression lead to apathy, anxiety, and irrationality.[4] Long bouts of depression trigger 'neurotransmitter switching,' affecting everything from emotions to perception. We will learn more about that in another chapter.

Some studies suggest that if a woman is suffering from depression during pregnancy, it can cause an enlargement of the amygdala during a baby's development in the womb. This has been linked to learning disabilities, behavioral issues, and emotional problems[5]. In this way, depression can become a generational curse passed on to our children, grandchildren, and beyond. Depression also appears to have a bi-directional relationship with neurological disorders. People with neurological disorders are more likely to develop depression, but depression seems to contribute to a higher risk of developing neurological disorders.[6]

Effects on the Body

Although depression is considered a brain disorder, it can have long-term and lasting effects on the body, both directly and indirectly. Depression is known to alter a person's appetite, leading to either eating less and causing unhealthy weight loss or eating more, resulting in unhealthy weight gain. Both situations can have serious negative effects if not addressed promptly. Depression has been indirectly linked to chronic pain, headaches, and even joint tenderness. It is possible that depression does not cause these issues, but rather, someone experiencing depression may be less tolerant of pain, making it more pronounced in a heightened sense of anxiety.

Depression triggers an overproduction of clotting factors, which can lead to heart disease and stroke. Since the gut is connected to mood and mental health, depression can cause gastrointestinal distress, resulting in symptoms such as stomach aches, indigestion, or bloating. Experiencing fatigue is a common symptom of depression[7]. Studies have shown that certain cancers are linked to depression[8]. It has been found that people with depression can suffer from 'psychosomatic disorder.' 'Psychosomatic disorder' is when a psychological condition leads to physical ailments, often with no medical explanation[9].

Internal Interconnectedness

I can remember days when I would experience tiredness (fatigue) to such a degree that my body would hurt. I could barely get out of bed, and most days, I did not want to. I was young and perfectly healthy, yet I had these symptoms. They were not imagined; I genuinely felt bad. However, these symptoms were a result of my psychology, not physiology. There came a time when those symptoms became a secondary gain for me. I justified to myself that if I felt bad, then I could take a 'me day.' I am not saying we should never take time to decompress or rest; it just cannot become a way of life. Living that way is unhealthy and creates more problems, which, in turn, perpetuates the same behavior.

When something is called 'psychosomatic,' it does not mean the symptoms are not real; they are not necessarily imagined. It just means that the source of the symptoms is not coming from a physical issue but from a psychological one. The word 'psycho' comes from the Greek word *psuche*, from which we get the word 'psyche'. Our psyche encompasses everything related to our minds, thoughts, and emotions. The word 'somatic' comes from the Greek word *soma*, which simply means our physical bodies. Therefore, when something is 'psychosomatic', it means that our minds, thoughts, and emotions are producing an effect in our bodies.

This implies that our minds and bodies are interconnected. We know the brain is linked to our nervous system, regulating physiological functions such as breathing, walking, eating, etc. However, our minds are a separate entity. Our minds reflect how we think, what we think, and how we perceive things. This unseen part of our being can affect the part of our being that we do see and experience. The Apostle Paul spoke about this in Hebrews 11:3: *"By faith, we understand that the worlds were framed by the word of God, so that the things which are seen were not made of things which are visible"* (NKJV). He is speaking about God, who is not physically visible, creating the visible world. But this also applies to our interconnectedness.

Perception

Another effect that depression has on us is how it shapes our perception. Depression distorts every input we receive. Constructive criticism transforms into judgment, truth becomes an attack, and someone not responding the way we anticipate turns into perceived hate. Situations are exaggerated when viewed through the lens of depression. It obscures our ability to see things properly and blinds us to solutions that may be right in front of us. There is a biblical account in Genesis that illustrates this perfectly—the story of Hagar and her son, Ishmael. In Genesis Fifteen, God promises Abram that he will have a son. In Genesis Sixteen, Abram's wife, Sarai, convinces him to have a child with her handmaid, Hagar, as Sarai was barren and believed this was the way God's promise would be fulfilled. Hagar conceives and gives birth to Abram's child, Ishmael.

In Genesis Seventeen, God informs Abram that His promise of a child will come through Sarai, and their names are changed to Abraham and Sarah to reflect this promise. Then, in Genesis Twenty-One, Sarah conceives and gives birth to Isaac, the child God promised her and Abraham. At one point, Ishmael mocks Isaac, and Galatians 4:29 states that Ishmael **persecuted** Isaac[10]. Sarah asks Abraham to send Hagar and Ishmael away. Abraham sends them away with a bottle of water and bread. Once the water and bread are gone, Hagar walks away from Ishmael so she won't have to witness him dying. As she sits, she begins to cry. In verse seventeen, an angel of the Lord tells her not to be afraid. Verse nineteen says, *"And God **opened her eyes**, and she saw a well of water; and she went, and filled the bottle with water, and gave the lad drink..."*

She saw a desperate situation. There seemed to be no hope. All she could do was cry. That is how depression works on us: it blinds us and keeps us paralyzed. Notice it says that God 'opened her eyes, and she saw a well of water.' It does not say God created the well; it says she was able to see it after being told not to fear. In other words, her emotions kept her from seeing what was right in front of her. God gives us a way of escape the same way He gave Hagar a way of escape.[11]

Are you willing to have your eyes opened?

15

Chapter 3
How Did I Get Here?

———•◇◇•———

As we move forward in this journey, we need to look at how the brain works. This will lead you to an understanding of how you arrived at the point of depression. You will observe how your brain operates in relation to how your mind processes information. We will focus on the 'how' instead of the 'why'. Any time we ask 'why,' we are seeking excuses. "Why did they do or say this?" "Why am I like this?" "Why do I do this?" These types of questions never resolve our issues; instead, they tend to reinforce and strengthen our emotions. 'Why' rarely, if ever, presents solutions; it merely highlights the problem. It is usually a question that arises out of frustration and self-condemnation.

Asking these types of questions typically results in attempting to assign blame. As long as we try to assign blame, even on ourselves, we never address the root issues. 'How' questions address solutions. They bring about responsibility because these questions aim to lead us to an understanding of the root causes that drive our problems. That is why this chapter is titled the way it is. If we can understand the **how,** or the workings that underpin the problems, then we can apply solutions to those problems. Think of it this way: if I know **how** something works, then I can do the opposite to achieve the desired result.

Remember, in Chapter Two, I mentioned that we would examine the root cause that leads to depression. I also mentioned that chemical imbalance is now recognized as a symptom rather than a cause of depression. Also, recall from Chapter One that other people and circumstances are not the cause of depression. So, if other people, negative circumstances, experiences, or chemical imbalances are the root causes that lead to depression, then what is the root cause of depression? It is how you think! More specifically, it is what we consistently focus on and meditate on. Researchers call it 'repetitive intrusive thoughts.'[1] 'Repetitive intrusive thoughts' are those thoughts that we **consistently** and habitually fall into.

We see, once again, that science is catching up and confirming what the Bible has told us for centuries. The first part of Proverbs 23:7 says, *"For as he thinketh in his heart, so is he...."* We produce things in our life according to what we think. We see a similar concept in 3 John 2, which says, *"Beloved, I wish above all things that thou mayest prosper and be in health, even as thy **soul** prospereth."* The word 'soul' in this verse is the Greek word *psuche*. We looked at this word in Chapter Two. It is where we get our English word *psyche*. It involves our minds, thoughts, and emotions[2]. This verse indicates that we experience positive things in life when our minds, thoughts, and emotions are fixed on positive things. Conversely, if we experience negative things, it would stand to reason that it is because our minds, thoughts, and emotions are fixed on negative things.

Notice that 3 John 2 also draws a correlation between the state of our soul and our health. This verse states that our mental health is directly tied to our physical health (psychosomatic). Scientists have confirmed this repeatedly over the years. Our thoughts are critically important to every part of our lives. The Bible mentions our thoughts in several places. Here are just a few, and we will look at more as we move forward in other chapters:

*Philippians 4:8 "Finally, brethren, whatsoever things are true, whatsoever things are honest, whatsoever things are just, whatsoever things are pure, whatsoever things are lovely, whatsoever things are of good report; if there be any virtue, and if there be any praise, **think on these things**."*

*Colossians 3:2 "Set your **minds** on things that are above, not on things that are on earth."*

2 Corinthians 10:5 "Casting down imaginations, and every high thing that exalteth itself against the knowledge of God, and **bringing into captivity every thought** *to the obedience of Christ;"*

Joshua 1:8 "This book of the law shall not depart out of thy mouth; but thou shalt **meditate** *therein day and night, that thou mayest observe to do according to all that is written therein: for* **then** *thou shalt make thy way* **prosperous***, and* **then** *thou shalt have* **good success***."*

Quantum Physics

We have all heard of the term 'quantum physics' or 'mechanics.' 'Quantum mechanics,' in simple terms, is the study of the field of atoms that make up physical matter. It is an unseen world. We cannot see it with our physical eyes. That field, which we cannot see, creates the world around us, which we can see. Quantum physics proves that the internal world is greater than the external world. It posits that the internal world creates and sustains the external world. Again, we see science catching up to the Bible. Hebrews 11:3 says, *"Through faith we understand that the worlds were framed by the word of God,* **so that things which are seen were not made of things which do appear.***"*

Quantum physics, like everything else, is part of a system of laws. For every natural law we see, there is a corresponding spiritual and individual law that applies. We see this in Romans 1:20, where it says, *"For the* **invisible** *things of him from the creation of the world are* **clearly seen***, being* **understood by the things that are made***, even his eternal power."* Spiritual laws are understood by observing natural laws. If natural law states that an internal world creates and sustains the physical world, then that law applies to us as well. What is happening within us—our thoughts and the way we process external data—will influence our physiology. Again, I will point out the concept in Proverbs 23:7: *"For as a man thinks, so is he….."*

19

The Effect of Thoughts In The Brain

Our thoughts are the root cause of our depression, but it goes a little deeper than that. Our thoughts are the catalyst for the way our brain is wired. That is why we can get locked into destructive patterns. Depression is not just psychological or emotional; it is physiological! The brain is made up of neurons that have tiny branches reaching out to other neurons, forming a **neural net**. The neurons in the brain are called 'pre-synaptic' and 'post-synaptic.' They are called 'synaptic' because communication between these neurons happens in the 'synaptic cleft,' a gap between the pre-synaptic and post-synaptic neurons. The pre-synaptic neurons fire off signals or impulses called neurotransmitters. These impulses are received by the post-synaptic neurons through the synaptic cleft[4].

The post-synaptic neuron has receptors that receive the signal from the neurotransmitter. The neurotransmitter will fire an electrical impulse, a signal, to the receptor when an emotion is experienced. That signal then follows the neural net, arriving at the hypothalamus. The hypothalamus will produce chemicals that match the signal sent from the receptor. These chemicals are called 'peptides'. The hypothalamus releases the peptides through the pituitary into the bloodstream. Once it hits the bloodstream, the peptides work through the body. Every cell has receptors that receive the peptide, similar to a key in a lock. The peptide sends a signal to that cell. Our body then experiences the physiological results of emotion that originated with a thought (psychosomatic).

Research shows that when we practice something repeatedly (repetitive actions and thinking), neurotransmitters and receptors form a long-term relationship. Since emotions cause the signal to be fired to the receptor, we must conclude that the chemicals released by that signal are influenced by our emotions. In turn, emotions are the by-product of thought and are triggered by thought. Therefore, how we think and what we think consistently determine what types of chemicals are produced. Research has also shown that repetitive thinking and actions determine **where** that chemical is released. It can change based on our thoughts. The term for this phenomenon is called 'neural switching' or 'neurotransmitter respecification'[6]. Hence, thoughts are the root cause of depression and can affect other issues such as physical ailments, neurological disorders, and other mental issues.

When the long-term relationship between neurons is influenced negatively, it creates an environment that we become dependent upon, even when we know our thinking and actions are unhealthy. The peptides released by the hypothalamus can change the cell, which can change the **needs** of that cell. This can make us dependent on that chemical, much like an addict. Studies have shown that heroin attaches to cell receptors the same way that peptides do. That is why it is so hard to break free from destructive or condemning behavior and thoughts: we are addicted to the chemicals released into our bloodstream. The cells need the peptides once they have been changed.

Jesus said it like this in John 8:34, *"Truly, truly, I say to you, everyone who practices sin is a **slave** to sin."* (ESV) The word 'practices' in this verse can also mean *habitually performs*. Paul presents the same concept in Romans 6. Romans 6:16 says *"Know ye not, that to whom ye **yield yourselves servants to obey**, his servants ye are to whom ye obey; whether of sin unto death, or of obedience unto righteousness?"* Romans 6:20 says *"For when ye were the servants of sin, ye were free from righteousness."* The concept presented here is that whatever we **habitually and consistently** practice is hardwired into us.

Remember, long-term relationships between neurons are formed through repetition. This implies that our repetitive thoughts and actions determine how our brains are wired and how the neural net is affected. Depression is the emotion produced by negative thoughts and faulty perceptions. That emotion is the catalyst for the chemicals produced in our body. We become trapped because we become used to those chemicals; we crave them, much like someone addicted to drugs. We become a slave. That is why it can be difficult to break free from things that we know are destructive.

How Did I Get Here?

So, to summarize, we arrived at the place of depression because we consistently and habitually thought about things that produced negative emotions. By focusing on those negative experiences, our brain created chemicals that were sent to the cells in our body. As those cells changed, they needed the chemicals produced by our emotions created by our thinking. It became a carousel: around and around we go. Every time we had repetitive thoughts, the cellular structure that was created got stronger and stronger. The truth is this: we created our own prison without even realizing it!

Now that we know how we got here, the next question is this: how do I get out of this cycle? Sometimes, we wonder if we can ever get off the carousel. I can tell you there is hope! We can break free from those repetitive thoughts and actions that hold us as prisoners.

Now that we know how we got here, let's look at how to get out of the cycle!

Chapter 4
Brain Healing

————•◇◇◇•————

We have established that our thoughts are the root cause of depression. Our thoughts produce emotions, which, in turn, send signals to our neural net. Over time, those signals change the hardwiring of our brain. We must understand that our brains were not designed with an inclination to depression. In other words, we are not born this way. There is no scientific evidence to support genetic causes of depression. Science does show that there is a distinct possibility of a natural disposition towards depression in people who have low self-esteem or who are overly critical of themselves. Research also shows that depression can run in families[1]. However, since there is no **genetic** evidence of depression, we must conclude that it is a **learned** behavior. We create it without even realizing it.

The hope for those struggling with depression is this: if depression is learned or developed, then it can be unlearned and undeveloped. If we are to break free from depression, we must change what we are doing that caused the cellular change. It may not be easy, but it is necessary. Your mind and body will resist you in the same way as an addict's mind and body will be resistant to any change. If our thoughts created the world we are experiencing, then we must start there. Remember what I said in the last chapter: if we can see **how** we arrived where we are currently, then we can reasonably conclude that doing the opposite will produce the results we desire. Most people want something different, but they refuse to take responsibility to make changes to bring about that different way of life.

Albert Einstein famously said, "The definition of insanity is doing the same thing over and over but expecting different results." Let's not apply insanity to an already complex issue. We must be willing to try something that we have not tried or have not been consistent in trying. Consistency is the key to changing all thoughts and actions. What we do **habitually** determines success or failure. One way to look at life issues is this: you did not get to where you are overnight, so you will not change it overnight. Consider this scripture in 2 Peter 2:7-8: *"And delivered just Lot,* **vexed** *with the filthy conversation of the wicked: (For that righteous man dwelling among them,* **in seeing and hearing, vexed his righteous soul from day to day** *with their unlawful deeds;)."* Lot's soul became 'vexed.' The words 'vexed' in these two verses have different meanings.

The first means 'to tire out or wear down[2].' The second means 'to torture[3].' Doesn't that sound just like depression? But notice that Lot became 'vexed' through **seeing and hearing from day to day.** In other words, it was consistent and habitual. The only way to overcome anything is to change the source. If our sins and other issues came through habitual practice, then overcoming our sins and issues must involve the habitual practice of the opposite of what caused our sins and issues. This holds true not only in thoughts but also in behavior. Whether it is alcoholism, drug addiction, pornography, gluttony, or even emotional issues, we must change what we are practicing.

The Cycle of Circular Health

Thoughts produce emotions. Emotions lead to actions and behavior, which, in turn, produce beliefs. Belief-based behavior then leads to reinforcing your thoughts, which produces the same emotions, resulting in the same actions and behavior, and so on and so forth. The term I use for this is 'circular health.' It is a cycle of repeating patterns that get stronger over time through the development of long-term relationships between the pre-synaptic and post-synaptic neurons. If we could see it in action, it would be a circle starting at the top with thoughts. The circle would move clockwise to emotions at 3 o'clock, actions and behavior at 6 o'clock, then to beliefs at 9 o'clock, and finally finish at the top once again with thoughts.

To break this cycle, an interruption of the cycle must occur. The interruption of the cycle occurs at the source: our thoughts. It sounds easy; just change your thoughts. It is a **simple** solution but not an **easy** solution to implement. As we have already seen, there are physiological and chemical realities at work against us. Adding to that, because of the long-term relationships that are formed in the neural net, we attach a significant amount of our identity, if not all our identity, to our beliefs that have been formed through our thoughts and associative memory. We have a hard time looking into the truth of our issues and interrupting the process due to the identity issue.

It is part of secondary gain. What am I without _____? I had a family member who constantly worried about everything. Throughout my entire life, I consistently heard this person talk about how worried they were about any given thing. Regardless of the situation or social setting, this person always brought the conversation around to their worry. During a visit with this person, they mentioned how concerned they were for their oldest son. This son had a good job, managed money very well, had a good life, and made good life decisions. I went through that with them and asked what there was to be worried about with this son. The reply was, "I just worry."

Then I mentioned that maybe they should stop worrying. The reply I received was, "If I stopped worrying, what would I do?" Their identity had become wrapped up in worrying about others and situations. They could not see life beyond being worried. They were addicted to worry. Sadly, this person developed cancer and passed away. I loved this family member very much. But the stress of carrying all that worry eventually killed them prematurely. This simple Biblical truth could have prevented that from happening: *Philippians 4:6-7 Do not be anxious about anything, but in every situation, by prayer and petition, with thanksgiving, present your requests to God. And the* **peace of God**, *which transcends all understanding, will* **guard your hearts and your minds** *in Christ Jesus.*

The Phenomenon Of Neuroplasticity

Breaking the cycle of negative circular health is vitally important. It affects the length of your life and the quality of life you experience. Scientists have found that the brain has an amazing ability to change and heal itself. This phenomenon is known as 'neuroplasticity'. Neuroplasticity is the healing or re-hardwiring of the brain in response to **mental** experience[4]. In other words, science now confirms that our thoughts can harm or heal our brain. Scientists once believed that the brain is fixed and unchangeable. We have already established that this belief has been proven incorrect. The brain can create new neural pathways. This involves breaking older long-term relationships and establishing newer, healthier long-term relationships between transmitters and receptors (pre-synaptic and post-synaptic neurons).

Neuroplasticity, the ability of the brain to heal, is dependent on 'neural switching,' the term we saw in Chapter Three. Neural switching changes long-term relationships between transmitters and receptors. It is the gain of one neurotransmitter and the loss of another in the same neuron in response to **chronic** stimulation[5]. In other words, as already mentioned several times, we gain and lose long-term relationships based on **what we think habitually and consistently**. Neuroplasticity proves what the Bible has said all along. *Proverbs 23:7* says, *"For as a man thinks, so is he...."* Science and the word of God place a huge emphasis on what we think as being vital to our life experiences. Changing our thinking changes our brain, which in turn changes the relationship between neurotransmitters, which in turn determines the chemical output to the neural net.

Renewing The Mind

Science calls brain healing 'neural switching' and 'neuroplasticity.' The Bible calls it **renewing the mind**. Romans 12:2 says, *"Do not be conformed to this world, but be **transformed** by the renewing of your mind...."* The word 'transformed' in the Greek is *metamorphoo*[6]. It is where we get our English word 'metamorphosis.' The picture that I see when I think of metamorphosis is of the caterpillar spinning itself into a cocoon. After a time of incubation, it emerges transformed into a butterfly. It goes from one state of being to the next. In the same way, we renew our minds to the will of God. The last part of Romans 12:2 says, *"Then you will be able to test and approve what is the good, pleasing, and perfect **will of God**."* So, renewing the mind is the process of learning the will of God.

The word 'renew' means *to renovate*[7]. When we renovate a house, we replace the old with something new. We are making it fresh. We are also making the house more comfortable and beautifying it. The root word for 'renew' in Greek means *repetition, intensity, and reversal.* You could say it like this: renewing the mind is an intense repetition that leads to a reversal. According to neural switching and neuroplasticity, we can reverse the effects that bad thinking and thought processes have produced in us. The question now becomes: what are we repeating intensely? What do we use to renew our minds to bring about brain healing? I will point you back to the last part of Romans 12:2: we renew our minds to the will of God.

Where do we find the will of God? We find it in His word! Research tells us that as we experience repetitive intrusive thoughts, we must interrupt the process to keep negative long-term relationships from forming in the neural net. One way that is advocated is called 'notice-shift-rewire'[8]. This method requires you to stop the train of thought and shift it in another direction. The Bible calls this 'guarding your heart.' Proverbs 4:23 says, *"Keep (guard) thy heart with all diligence; For out of it are the issues of life."* The missing piece to this process is this: what do we shift our focus upon? We shift our focus to the word of God! Since the word of God is the 'lamp unto our feet' (Psalm 119:105), then we must shift to that.

Remember Joshua 1:8: *"This book of the law shall not depart out of thy mouth; but thou shalt **meditate** therein **day and night**, that thou mayest **observe** to do according to all that is written therein: for **then** thou shalt make thy way prosperous, and **then** thou shalt have good success."* It is not enough to just simply shift our focus. The focus of the shifting is equally as important, if not more so. We see an example of this in Matthew 4:1-

10 and Luke 4:1-12. It is the account of Jesus' temptation in the wilderness. Each time satan brought a temptation to Jesus, He countered it with God's word. Jesus did not simply shift focus. He shifted focus to the 'bread of life.'[9] Renewing the mind is not just thinking differently. It is habitually and consistently thinking about the word of God.

It is also the process of learning the word. You cannot meditate on what you do not know. You cannot shift to something that is not there. The process starts with learning the word. You may need to cut off the television and prioritize what you need to do to learn. Go to a good church and get involved. When you are involved, you are invested. When you are invested, you pay better attention to the preaching and teaching of the word. Remember, you are renovating through repetition. Something that irks me is when people say they want to hear something new. "Oh, the pastor has taught on this for weeks now. Let's move on to something new." They do not understand the renewing of the mind. Intense **repetition** brings a reversal. I love what Paul said in Philippians 3:1: *"Finally, my brethren, rejoice in the Lord. To write the **same** things to you, to me indeed is **not** grievous, but for you it is **safe**."*

Recovering Sight

Intrusive thoughts are contrary to the word of God. When these thoughts occur, we must shift to what God says in those situations. We cannot continue to focus on intrusive thoughts. If we do persist in focusing on those thoughts, our emotions become overwhelmed. These emotions flood our entire being with chemicals that are distributed throughout our body. When we begin to feel overwhelmed in situations and thoughts, we must interrupt the process before it has time to take root in us. In Mark 6, we find the account of one instance of Jesus feeding a multitude with five loaves of bread and two fish. In verse 41, it says that He *"looked up to heaven."*[10] That phrase in Greek means 'to recover sight.'[11] Jesus was in an overwhelming situation, and He stopped to recover sight. He did not allow the situation to influence His thoughts. Notice it says He looked to **heaven** to recover sight. **Where** we place our focus is just as important as interrupting the process itself. If Jesus had to stop and recover sight, then so must we.

One way we recover sight is through the act of praise and worship. As the cares of life and intrusive thoughts weigh on us, we can stop what we are doing and thinking and redirect our focus back to God. In this way, we honor God above our thoughts and emotions. Instead of becoming overwhelmed with our situation, we look to the source of life and His help. Hebrews 4:16 says, *"Let us then come with confidence to the throne of grace, that we may obtain mercy and find grace to help in time of need."* What better time to find 'grace to help' than when we need to recover sight?

Hebrews 13:15   "By him therefore let us offer the sacrifice of praise to God continually, that is, the fruit of our lips giving thanks to his name."

Place Of Repentance

Another Biblical concept for this process is repentance. The primary Greek word for repentance (*metanoeo*) simply means 'to think differently, to reconsider, to change our mind.'[12] This Greek word is the root for another Greek word used for repentance, *metanoia*.[13] This second Greek word implies a reversal of a decision that leads to reformation or change. It begins with changing our minds or our thoughts. Changing our thoughts, in turn, changes our brain; they contribute to its healing. If we desire brain healing and a transformation in our lives, we must renew, recover, and repent.

Renewing, recovering, and repenting are keys to brain healing!

Chapter 5
Enemies In Our Minds

————◦◇◇◦————

Our psychological processes are directly correlated with our physiological processes. In other words, we become what we think. The early scientific belief was that our genetic makeup was responsible for our perceptions and behaviors. I am sure we have all used the excuse, or heard someone use the excuse, of 'this is just the way I am.' This excuse is as old as mankind itself. Then science seemed to confirm this belief. But research in recent years has shown that our thoughts are more of the driver for perceptions and behaviors than heredity.[1] In the first concept, we are slaves to a force outside of our control: DNA. In the second concept, we have more control over our lives. Romans 6:16 shows us that the second concept is the truth: we yield ourselves![2]

If we have more control through our thoughts, rather than little to no control through heredity, then more emphasis must be placed on the environment in which we consistently find ourselves. When we are children, we have very little control over our environment. Since most science in the field of psychology defaults to genetics and/or blame-shifting, very few people come to this scriptural conclusion: we, and we alone, are responsible for our lives before man and God. As we have established so far, the word of God is the standard of truth. God's word says in 1 Corinthians 15:33, *"Be not deceived: evil communications corrupt good manners."* In other words, our environment has more to do with the results of our lives than anything else. We think a certain way because we have been trained through association, perception, and experience to think that way.

31

I am not suggesting that DNA has no influence on us at all. I am suggesting that DNA has very little influence compared to our thoughts. We can absolutely be slaves to our DNA, but only if we allow it to be so. Likewise, we can be slaves to our environment as well. The mind is our own worst enemy in most cases. However, our mind can also be our greatest asset if we channel its focus properly. Thinking negatively causes us to experience the 'nocebo effect.' The 'nocebo effect' is the result of a negative thought. Thinking positively causes us to experience the 'placebo effect.' The 'placebo effect' is the result of a positive thought[3]. Both ways of thinking produce effects in every aspect of our lives. Proverbs 15:13 says, *"A joyful* **(positive)** *heart makes a face cheerful, but a sad* **(negative)** *heart produces a broken spirit."* (HCSB) Proverbs 17:22 says, *"A cheerful* **(positive)** *heart is good medicine, but a crushed* **(negative)** *spirit dries up the bones."* (NLT)

Becoming What We Think

Every cell in our body is aware of our thoughts and feelings. Due to the way we are created, these thoughts and feelings generate physiological responses that work to manifest those thoughts and feelings. An example of this is 'psychosocial dwarfism.' In the study of this phenomenon, children who believe they are unloved will experience depleted levels of growth hormones[4]. As mentioned earlier, our thoughts lead to emotions; we then act or behave based on those emotions. This behavior creates a belief, reinforcing the original thought. If someone thinks they are undeserving of a caring relationship, the associated emotion will lead to behavior that simultaneously attracts uncaring people and repels caring people. This emotion will manifest in body language, vocal tone, words, and decisions.

This phenomenon is known as a 'self-fulfilling prophecy' and is the result of what you truly believe about yourself and the world around you. It originates from a place that science refers to as 'the subconscious mind.' While the term is familiar to most of us, it is not a new concept in science. Involuntary neurological responses, such as

32

breathing, eye blinking, and heart pumping, are governed by the subconscious mind. Scientists have known for decades that the subconscious mind is more powerful than the conscious mind[5]. What science terms the subconscious mind, the Bible refers to as 'the heart.' Proverbs 4:23 says, *"Keep thy heart with all diligence; for out of it are the issues of life."* The New International Version says it this way: *"Above all else, **guard** your heart for everything you do flows from it."*

Research has shown that the heart, or subconscious mind, sends out signals around us that influence, attract, and repel[6]. We not only become what we think; we influence the world around us through our thoughts[7]. More specifically, what we **believe** is the primary driver of what is produced in us and around us. The Word of God says that we are to guard our heart above all else because out of **our heart** flow the issues of life. What we consistently and habitually allow ourselves to think determines not only our physiology but also our life experiences. This principle is applicable in every aspect of life. If we think negatively long enough, we experience depression, which affects our physiology, including our health. Consequently, we then experience life through that belief-reinforced awareness. The same holds true if we consistently focus on sickness, as a belief that we are sick forms out of it.

I remember a man I knew years ago who has since gone on to be with the Lord. For as long as I knew him, he would consistently say, "My mother died of cancer, my father died of cancer, my brother died of cancer, my sister died of cancer, so I will die of cancer." He had lung cancer before I met him, and he had a lung removed. Just a few short years after meeting him, he was diagnosed with another form of cancer. It was a cancer that typically grew slowly and could be treated. However, he was gone within less than six months after the diagnosis. His belief accelerated the growth, and the doctors commented that it should not have spread that quickly. Every cell in our body works to produce what we believe. Again, our beliefs are formed initially as thoughts, and they only become beliefs through the repetition of thought and behavior. Psalm 139:14 says we are fearfully and wonderfully made[8], which takes on new meaning in this context.

Meditation Creates Our Orientation

The psalmist said this in Psalm 19:14, *"Let the **words of my mouth**, and the **meditation of my heart**, be acceptable in thy sight, O LORD, my strength, and my redeemer."* What we think and what we say are tied together. The words of my mouth **are** the meditation of my heart. Jesus said it like this in Matthew 12:34, *"for out of the abundance of the heart the mouth speaketh."* You will say whatever you believe in your heart, or subconscious mind. If you think about something long enough, you begin to believe it in your heart. Then you say that belief, hear yourself say it, and it becomes reinforced in your heart. Those long-term relationships are formed in the neural net, and away we go. Meditation is simply deeply pondering something. People hear the word 'meditation,' and it conjures up images of burning incense and chanting. But really, meditation is just deeply thinking about something.

Everyone meditates on something, even if they do not use that specific terminology. People say things like, "I'm sick with worry," or, "I am trying to wrap my mind around it." Those are just different ways of saying they are meditating. As the psalmist says, we want our words and thoughts to be acceptable to God. What is acceptable to God is that our words and thoughts be in line with God's Word. Why are words so important in influencing our heart? Words are spoken thoughts. Thoughts are powerful enough by themselves; we have already seen that. But when spoken, they carry a lot more force. Proverbs 18:21 says it like this: *"Death and life are in the power of the tongue, and they that love it shall eat the fruit thereof."* Death and life are in the power of the tongue—our words! Notice the end of this verse: 'eat the fruit thereof' means we reap the consequences of our words.

James 3:5-6 *"Even so the **tongue** is a little member, and boasteth great things. Behold, how great a matter a little fire kindleth! And the tongue is a **fire**, a world of **iniquity**: so is the tongue among our members, that it **defileth the whole body**, and **setteth on fire the course of nature**; and it is set on fire of hell."* Jesus said that we would make an account of every idle word in the day of judgment, or the day of our decision[9]. In other words, what

34

we say affects every aspect of our life. Our words and thoughts bring us to a place where we reap what we sow. Joshua 1:8 talks about meditating in the word of God day and night, or habitually and consistently. The Hebrew word for 'meditate' in that verse means to ponder **and** to utter. In other words, what we think and what we say. Meditation creates our orientation!

Perception

Another way our mind becomes our enemy is in our perception. How we define things is how we relate to those things, and these definitions shape our perception. The neural net in our brains operates on the 'law of associative memory.' Our definitions are formed from experiences, whether something we heard, saw, or physically experienced. As issues and situations enter our lives, they pass through the filter of 'associative memory.' Consequently, we relate to current situations based on associative memory—not necessarily what is truly happening but our perception of what is happening. The Bible refers to this as 'judgment'. Jesus addresses this concept in Matthew 7[11]. When we apply judgment, we impose our perception onto a situation or question others' motives. This process is not based on truth but on our view derived from our experiences.

I recall a time when my wife and I were a young married couple. She would bring things to my attention that needed correction for my growth and maturity. However, I would often become angry with her, interpreting all criticism as an attack. Similarly, when my pastor pointed out areas for my growth, I would feel depressed. What the Lord showed me was that I had an associative memory of criticism and had developed a defense mechanism against it. In my youth, authority figures and people I trusted spoke negatively about me, insisting I would never amount to anything and labeling me as a bad person. Consequently, my emotions formed a defense mechanism to shield me from what I perceived as a personal attack. When individuals who genuinely cared for me highlighted areas for improvement, my perception was that they were trying to hurt or limit me. I filtered their motives through my perception, shaped by associative memory, assuming that the motives behind constructive criticism were the same as hurtful criticism.

When we default to perception through associative memory, we miss the bigger picture. We remember events according to how we perceive them, and we almost always perceive things in a way that aligns with a pre-determined belief; this is known as a 'bias.' A 'bias' is simply how we are inclined to think about someone or something, including ourselves. Our biases determine how we perceive things, potentially distorting a situation and preventing us from seeing the truth. A bias causes us to only consider information that supports that inclination. The brain processes four hundred billion bits of information per second, yet we are consciously aware of only two thousand bits of information per second. We eliminate the other information so that what remains is the information that is the most self-serving or confirms our biases.

If I think I am a bad person, if that is my bias or inclination, then I will focus on information that supports that belief and eliminate the rest. The same is true in the opposite direction. This is one reason so many people fail to grow in their lives; they reject critical information that could potentially help them. Instead, they focus on bias and perception, dwelling on those thoughts and wiring their brain toward a pre-determined outcome. They cause that outcome to happen from their heart and then say, "See, I told you so." When we do that, we reject objective truth and embrace subjective truth, or as we say in our culture today, 'my truth.' We do the same with other people: we relate to them through our perception and bias, remembering events, even current events, through our perception and bias.

Living out of perception and bias will ultimately lead us to a place of depression. I have seen this in my own life, and I have observed it in the lives of others. Our focus becomes self-centered as we filter others' actions through how they affect us, saying things like, "They are doing this to **me**!" or "This is how they make **me** feel." Alternatively, we may filter everything through either a negative perception or an inflated perception of our identity, saying things like

"**I** am a bad person" or "How could they do this to **me**?" These extremes of self-centeredness result from living out of perception and bias. Without fail, I have observed that when we reach this place of skewed perspective, depression follows.

In the chapters ahead, we will explore different ways of thinking and the adjustments needed to be free to see the truth. We will also begin to examine habits that lead to depression and the Biblical principles to overcome and change those habits. You may find that you fall into only one or two of these habits or perhaps several or even all of them. Keep in mind that habits that do not seem to apply to you can still provide valuable insights. When you identify these issues, you are on your way to overcoming them!

We can change our reality by changing what we think in line with God's word!

Chapter 6
Shame and Condemnation

————•◇△◇•————

The first thing we will look at regarding thoughts and habits that lead to depression is the Biblical concepts of shame and condemnation. For the believer, dealing with these is of the utmost importance because shame and condemnation are tied directly to a negative perception of ourselves, God, and our relation to, and interaction with, God. Condemnation is one of the Biblical terms for depression. 1 John 3:20 says, *"For if our heart condemn us, God is greater than our heart, and knoweth all things."* Notice that 1 John 3:20 says, "if our heart condemns us". A key point going forward here is that God is not the author of condemnation; our hearts are the source of condemnation. In John 3:17, Jesus says this: *"For God did not send his Son into the world to condemn the world, but that the world through him might be saved."* The Lord Jesus Himself declares that God is not the condemner. Condemnation is an inside job. It comes from our hearts. Condemnation is driven by shame. Shame, from a Biblical definition, is a sense of lack. One Hebrew definition for shame, or ashamed, means to be dry[1]; you could also say to be thirsty or empty. It means we are without something.

We can see shame being introduced to mankind very early in Genesis Chapter Three, in the account of the sin of Adam; also known as the fall of man. First, let's look at Genesis 2:25, it says, *"And they were both naked, the man and his wife, and were not ashamed."* Then we read in Genesis 3:7-8, after Adam and Eve ate the fruit of the tree of the knowledge of good and evil, *"And the eyes of them both were opened, and they knew that they were naked; and they sewed fig leaves together and made themselves aprons. And they heard the voice of the Lord God walking in the garden in the cool of the day: and Adam and his wife hid themselves from the presence of the Lord God amongst the trees of the garden."* The very first effect of sin was shame. In Genesis 2:25, they were naked but not ashamed, or felt no lack. In Genesis 3:7, they saw their nakedness and felt a lack. We know this because they covered themselves with fig leaves. They were trying to cover what they felt they were lacking. In Genesis 3:8, we see the result of shame in the form of condemnation. After covering themselves, they hid from God. This is what condemnation produces: alienation from God's life and presence, which also means cutting ourselves off from the source of our solutions.

Shame is a perception. We perceive that we are lacking something. As we have already established, perceptions (what and how we think) produce emotions, then emotions produce actions, and actions form beliefs. Actions produced to compensate for lack are what the Bible calls 'walking after the flesh.' We see this clearly in Romans 8:1, which says, *"There is therefore now no condemnation to them which are in Christ Jesus, who walk not after the flesh but after the Spirit."* Notice that Romans 8:1 does not say there is no condemnation at all. It says there is no condemnation for those who do not walk after the flesh but walk after (or in) the spirit. This implies there is condemnation for those who "walk after the flesh."

Another Biblical term for these shame-based actions is 'dead works'[2], or 'our righteousness(es).'[3] They are dead works because we are trying to do what only God can do for us. They are dead because they will not work and will produce condemnation, which is a form of death. The more we try to overcome what we perceive as a lack in ourselves through our strength, the more we fall into condemnation or depression. Our heart knows that we can never do enough to overcome our sense of lack. Condemnation can be defined as the expectation of rejection and punishment. It convinces us that we are worthless and that God is rejecting us. That is the belief produced in Adam and Eve after they sinned in the Garden of Eden. Shame produces condemnation. Keep in mind, though, that condemnation is not from God; it originates in our perception which is then produced in our heart.1 John 3:20, which we saw earlier, confirms that.

1 John 3:21 says, *"Beloved, if our heart condemn us not, then have we confidence toward God."* If our hearts do not condemn us, it produces confidence with God. Conversely, if our hearts do condemn us, then we must reasonably conclude that we will not have confidence with God. The word 'confidence' in Greek implies a confidence that produces openness and freedom before the Lord.[4] It is the exact opposite of what Adam and Eve felt in the Garden of Eden after their sin. It is where God wants us to be with Him: in faith. Hebrews 4:13 says, *"Neither is there any creature that is not manifest in his sight: but all things are* **naked and opened** *unto the eyes of him with whom we have to do."* But if we continue to operate out of a sense of lack, we will withhold ourselves from His presence. Our hearts will condemn us, and we will lose confidence with God. His will is that we *"come boldly unto the throne of grace, that we may obtain mercy, and find grace to help in time of need."* (Hebrews 4:16)

The Difference Between Guilt and Condemnation

People often confuse guilt with condemnation. There is a difference between guilt and condemnation. Guilt is a temporary emotion; condemnation is a belief that produces a more permanent state of being. Left unchecked, guilt will lead to condemnation. Guilt can be an effective tool for change if that emotion will lead us to positive actions. The Bible calls guilt 'godly sorrow.' 2 Corinthians 7:10 says, *"For godly sorrow worketh repentance to salvation not to be repented of: but the sorrow of the world worketh death."* Guilt can work repentance (reversal, change of mind) if we act on it quickly and do not let it fester in our minds. How do we act quickly? What is it we do when we feel guilt, or godly sorrow? We run to God first and ask for mercy and help. The quicker we run to Him, the better off we will be. The longer we avoid Him, the quicker we fall into condemnation. Condemnation will cause us to run from God, but godly sorrow will bring us to Him if we can keep our emotions tempered.

Hebrews 4:16 "Let us therefore come boldly unto the throne of grace, that we may obtain mercy, and find grace to help in time of need."

1 John 1:9 "If we confess our sins, he is faithful and just to forgive us our sins, and to cleanse us from all unrighteousness."

Shame and condemnation are our enemies!

Chapter 7
Hope and Faith

————◇◇◇————

We have already established that once we diagnose a problem, the solution is to simply apply the opposite of the problem to overcome it. Shame and condemnation can only be overcome with hope and faith; hope and faith are the opposites of shame and condemnation. Shame and condemnation have their roots in faulty perceptions and feelings about God, which bleed over into the rest of our lives. Hope and faith have their roots in seeing God through Biblical truth apart from feelings; seeing God as He defines Himself. Shame is a sense of lack; hope is a sense of provision. Hope, defined in Greek, is the confident expectation of good.[1] Condemnation is the expectation of rejection and punishment; it is mistrusting God. Faith is the expectation of God's goodness; it is trusting God. Remember what we have established so far: our brains and bodies work to produce what we think and perceive. If we think God is mad and judging us, we will look at everything that confirms that bias and reject the rest. This is why it is so important to build on the word of God and not our emotions.

I can remember when I first saw these Biblical concepts of hope and faith. I was so condemned because I did not feel 'good enough.' I was born-again, but I felt that God had rejected me because of sin and bad attitude. How did I break free? I came to the realization through the word of God that God is good, and He is not rejecting me! I let the Bible change my perceptions! I replaced what I was thinking with the word of truth. It is never enough to just change the subject of your thoughts; to derail the train, so to speak. Jesus talked about a man who had been freed of an unclean spirit. After some time passed, that spirit came back to the 'house.' The 'house' was empty, clean, and decorated. But the spirit entered back in and brought more unclean spirits with it.[2] Notice the house was clean but empty. We do not just change the subject of our thoughts; we replace them with God's word.

If we are walking in shame and condemnation, we must cut off the thinking and perceptions that brought us to this point. Since shame is a sense or perception of lack, we must repent and renew our minds to what God's word says about provision. We must find the scriptures that talk about the good things God has given to us. As we change our perceptions about lack, hope takes root in our hearts and faith is produced. Hebrews 11:1 says, *"Now faith is the substance of things hoped for, the evidence of things not seen."* Faith is the substance, what is produced, by hope: expecting good things from God. If I expect good things from God, I can trust Him. Hope and faith must be established or built within your heart. In the context of God's goodness, Romans 10:17 says, *"So then faith cometh by hearing, and hearing by the word of God."* When you listen to preachers and teachers, you hear it. When you think it, you hear it. When you say it, you hear it. Faith comes by hearing.

When my eyes were finally opened to see hope and faith, I searched the scriptures for the good things of God. I am encouraging you to do the same. Find them, think on them, say them! I would recommend finding resources that have those laid out. It will help you speed up the process. I have a resource available, a book called 'Psalm 19:14 Setting My Heart: Scriptures To Renew The Mind and Establish The Heart.' It has four major areas of scriptures that we cover that will help you build hope and faith, and a couple of bonus sections as well. You can find it on Amazon and my website: www.randallrittenberry.com. In the meantime, here are a few to get you started.:

2 Peter 1:3-4 "His divine power has given us everything we need for a godly life through our knowledge of him who called us by his own glory and goodness. Through these he has given us his very great and precious promises, so that through them you may participate in the divine nature, having escaped the corruption in the world caused by evil desires." (NIV)

Romans 8:31-32 "What then shall we say to these things? If God is for us, who can be against us? He who did not spare His own Son, but delivered Him up for us all, how shall He not with Him also freely give us all things?" (MEV)

Philippians 4:19 "But my God shall supply all your need according to his riches in glory by Christ Jesus."

God reveals His character and attributes through His name. In John 17:6, Jesus said that He revealed God's **name**.[3] We see throughout the Old Testament that God would reveal something about Himself by adding that attribute of His character to His name. One of those names is Jehovah-Jireh, the God who provides.[4] Jesus said in John 10:10, *"The thief cometh not, but for to steal, and to kill, and to destroy: I am come that they might have life, and that they might have it more **abundantly**."* It is God's desire to provide for us. When our hearts become established that we have no lack in Christ, hope arises, and faith takes root. Shame and condemnation lose power over us!

The Power of Thankfulness

One Biblical principle for building and maintaining hope and faith is thankfulness. Thankfulness focuses on what we **do** have, instead of focusing on what we **do not** have. When we are not thankful, it is easy for shame (a sense of lack) to enter our thoughts. Romans 1:21 describes the effects of not being thankful: *"Because that, when they knew God, they glorified him not as God, neither were **thankful**; but became vain in their imaginations, and their foolish heart was darkened."* The Greek word for 'darkened' means *to darken, obscure*.[5] When something is obscured, it means it is not in plain sight. In other words, we do not see clearly. The word 'vain' in this verse means *empty* or *foolish, futile*.[6] This is an accurate description of being depressed. There is a feeling of darkness that comes over our thoughts and emotions. It feels like everything is pointless (futile[7]). Frustration is at every turn. In truth, we are simply not seeing clearly. Thankfulness brings back focus.

Ephesians 4:17 tells us not to walk in the vanity of our mind.[8] Vain imaginations are thoughts that produce nothing good. Jonah 2:8 says, *"They that observe **lying vanities** forsake their own mercy."* When we are in a place where we are not seeing clearly, and we continue to speak and think things about our lives that are not true, we will not be able to find mercy. It did not say that God was not extending mercy; it says we forsake that mercy. We ignore the help God is trying to give to us. 1 Corinthians 10:13 says that God makes a way of escape from our temptation.[9] When our vision and outlook are darkened, we will not see the way of escape. We will reject the principles He gives us in scripture that would help us escape. When we lose hope, nothing presented to us will seem as though it will help. Our minds get wrapped up in worry to the point that our hearts become darkened. Becoming darkened does not mean we become evil; it means we cannot see clearly. Thankfulness keeps us focused on what God has done and will do for us.

The Power of Remembrance

Thankfulness, in a lot of ways, is like the memorials that the Lord would have the Israelites build whenever He did something for them. They would build an altar and name the place according to what God had done for them there. In this way, they would always have a reminder to themselves and generations to come of what the Lord had done for them. Similarly, when we take time to thank God for things He has done for us, it reminds us of the help and blessings we have from Him. Each of us can think of several things God has done for us. It is a powerful thing for our faith. 2 Peter 1:13 says, *"I consider it right, as long as I live in this body, to stir you up by reminding you,"* (MEV) Thankfulness stirs us up. It keeps hope and faith alive. As long as hope and faith are alive, shame and condemnation cannot thrive. Thankfulness and remembrance are vital keys to victory!

1 Corinthians 15:57 "But thanks be to God, which giveth us the victory through our Lord Jesus Christ."

46

1 Thessalonians 5:18 "In everything give thanks: for this is the will of God in Christ Jesus concerning you."

Hope and faith overcome shame and condemnation!

Thankfulness and remembering God's blessings help us build hope and faith!

Chapter 8
Mental Movies

———◆◇◆———

Have you ever had a memory resurface seemingly out of nowhere? Before you know it, that memory is playing out in your mind. You let it unfold just as if you are watching a show on television. These are what I call 'mental movies.' They are memories on which you have placed significant value. They are usually memories that have created a strong emotional response at the time it happened. Typically, these memories reinforce heart beliefs, and the mind is working to seek justification for those beliefs. This is an issue I dealt with for many years. I would replay memories of events and incidents that took place as far back as when I was four or five years old. I never knew when a memory would trigger. It literally seemed to come out of nowhere. That is the way it seems to be, but what is really happening is what we discussed in Chapter Five: the 'law of associative memory.' You see or hear something that triggers that memory. Your mind associates something currently happening with what has happened in the past.

When that happens, the mental movies begin to play. Anytime we see, hear, or experience something, it elicits emotional and physiological responses. Keep in mind that the brain does not know the difference between what is currently happening and what it remembers. To the brain, a current event and a memory hold the same value. When you replay the mental movies, the emotions and physiological responses you experienced the first time that event occurred, you will experience during the replay. To the brain, that memory is happening in real time. It holds both the event itself and the responses you experienced. When you replay it, you experience the responses again. The same parts of your brain are triggered in memory as in real-time. Not only that, but you will experience those responses more intensely. Jesus said it like this in Mark 4:24, *"And He said to them, Be careful what you are hearing. The measure [of thought and study] you give [to the truth you hear] will be the measure [of virtue and knowledge] that comes back to you—and* **more** *[besides] will be given to you who hear."*

Jesus said the more thought you give to something, the **more** it will come back to you. So, the responses you experience in mental movies are increased compared to the original event. The reason for this is that we superimpose our perception and judgment on top of that memory. We not only experience the original responses but also the responses that are created by how we perceive what happened and why we think it happened. The mind will also superimpose the responses of past replays of any memory. If you have a memory that you have replayed a dozen times, then those emotions and physiological responses are at least twelve times more intense than the original event. It is just how the mind works. Each replay increases our emotional response, which in turn increases the chemicals released into the pituitary. They say that time heals all wounds, but that is not the case with our thoughts and emotions. They do not heal if we continue to replay them. They will deepen and intensify.

Letting Go of The Past

Mental movies are deeper than repetitive, intrusive thoughts. While those thoughts can become a source of oppression if left unchecked, repetitive, intrusive thoughts can be overcome by cutting them off as soon as they come across your mind. Mental movies are memories of actual events. They have created a mark in your mind that has influenced nearly every aspect of your life. The consequences of those events, and then the reliving of those events, will produce more limitations in your heart than nearly anything else. As I mentioned earlier, we have placed significant value on these events and allowed them to influence our perception and judgment due to the value we placed on them. They will also produce more conflict with others as we relate to others out of the associative memory, perceptions, and judgments we have formed. What we must remember is that these things are **in the past**. There is absolutely nothing we can do to change those events.

The only thing that remains with any incident or event is what can be learned in the moment, and how we decide to proceed. Once we attach value to an event, we are locked into the perceptions and judgments of that event. We then enter that cycle of circular health we saw in an earlier chapter. Look at what the Apostle Paul said about the past in Philippians 3:13-14: *"Brethren, I count not myself to have apprehended: but this one thing I do, **forgetting those things which are behind, and reaching forth** unto those things which are before, I press toward the mark for the prize of the high calling of God in Christ Jesus."* In other words, Paul is saying I am not going to camp out on what is behind. Not that we cannot learn from things that happen and grow from them. We just are not going to place an inordinate amount of time and effort on things we cannot change; nor are we going to allow those things to define us by placing an exaggerated importance on them. When we do, we become limited by that event every time we replay it in our mind's eye.

The Root of Bitterness

The longer we dwell on the past, the longer it takes us to get where God wants to take us. The Apostle Paul said, "I reach forth and press toward the prize of the high calling of God." You cannot reach forth if you are looking back. You must let it go. If you are hanging on to sorrow from past behavior, let it go. If you are hanging on to past hurts from others, let it go. The longer we hang onto the past, the longer we delay being set free. We will remain bitter and depressed. Bitterness feeds depression. The degree to which you replay mental movies is the degree to which you are bitter about those events, whether towards yourself or others. The Bible calls it 'the root of bitterness': *Hebrews 12:15 "Looking diligently lest any man fail of the grace of God; lest any root of bitterness springing up trouble you, and thereby many be defiled;"* Bitterness is the result of not letting go of past hurts. The preceding verse in Hebrews speaks of following peace with all men.[1] So, the context of not allowing bitterness is to find peace within ourselves. Internal peace comes by letting things go; we can only let go when we remove value from that event, which in turn frees us from judgment and perception.

Notice that Hebrews 12:15 says that the root of bitterness can cause 'many to be defiled'. When we allow bitterness to take root, it affects others as well. The Greek word for 'defiled' means *to contaminate, to pollute*[2]. Bitterness contaminates and pollutes everything and everyone around us. When we are bitter or hurting, it comes out on those around us. As the saying goes, "Hurting people hurt people." I can remember the day that I had to deal with bitterness and hurt that I had carried nearly my entire life. My father was a source of pain for me. He had a drinking problem and extreme anger issues. I was constantly belittled. There were good times as well. I do not want to paint a picture that is not accurate. Regardless of the good times, the hurt was still there. I carried this into my adult life, and that root of bitterness created in me the same anger issues my father carried. On my thirtieth birthday, I was praying and telling the Lord that I did not understand why my father had done and said the things that had hurt me.

The Lord told me, in no uncertain terms, that those things were not done **to me**. I got angry with God when he said that. He then explained to me that my father carried hurt and bitterness, and nothing was directed at me. I was just in the way. Although my father's intent was not to hurt anybody, his root of bitterness hurt, or polluted and contaminated, others. Because of his bitterness, I became bitter. The root of bitterness was well on its way to becoming a generational curse in my family. Once I understood that what had happened was not personal, I was able to forgive and let go. That curse stopped at me. If I had continued in that bitterness, I would have polluted and contaminated everything and everyone around me. I could have possibly lost the people in my life that I love and care about, and who love and care about me. It could easily have been a trap for my life. Thank God for His wisdom and mercy!

The root of bitterness does not have to destroy your life!

Chapter 9
Faulty Expectations

———•◇◇◇•———

We cannot look at dealing with depression and not address the subject of faulty expectations. A faulty expectation is when we expect others to meet needs that they are not designed to meet. It can also be when we create expectations from others without their consent. It is a sub-conscious expectation that is generally driven by internal principles from past experiences, almost a self-defense mechanism. When we operate from faulty expectations, we place great pressure on others. That pressure wears people out mentally and emotionally. They are made to feel guilty for not meeting a particular need in the way we believe that they should. Sometimes, it is not guilt, but a constant nagging of subtle criticism. I have seen this happen so much that I can identify it quickly. Instead of being happy when someone is willing to take time for them, they instead gripe that it is not enough, no one cares for them, and so on. They will then get offended when the people they criticize no longer want to be around them. They will say, "No one wants to see me." They are right, but they overlook that they have created that attitude themselves.

In these days of social media, we see this phenomenon clearly. Someone will make a post about what is wrong with them or play the victim. Some may say that it is a cry for help, but it is not; rather, it is a manipulation of others to gain comfort. They are using others to try to gain what only God can provide. They are substituting growth for temporary comfort and may receive temporary comfort from some people. However, as soon as someone presents the truth, they become offended. In their minds and emotions, they perceive themselves as victims. Again, they may be right, but they have created this situation.

Depression sets in as the emotion of victimhood sets in. The self-talk begins in their minds, and they fall into a cycle of circular behavior. When offense arises because others cannot or will not be what we think they should be, we find ourselves in the trap of faulty expectations. Just as we assign value to memories, we also assign value to people. In that scenario, people become idols to us, replacing God in our heart.

Emotion Vampires

This is known in counseling circles as co-dependency. We become dependent on others for our emotional needs, turning into 'emotion vampires' always on the lookout for someone from whom we can draw life. Here is a way to spot this behavior: emotion vampires change friends and running buddies quite often; they are constantly on the move. They must do this as they exhaust people quickly. A Biblical term for this behavior is 'being a wolf.'[1] Wolves are always looking for the weak and distracted to feed upon. They will find people who genuinely want to love and help others, then take advantage of them. The entire premise is built on what is offered from others, not what can be given to others. It is self-centered. They will shame others when they do not get their way and try to convince them they are not showing love. It is all a manipulation to get their way. In this scenario, depression is always at the doorstep. Many times, depression is used as a tool to draw others in. I am not saying it is not real; just that a wolf has learned how to use their emotions to identify stray sheep.

I am convinced that most people are not aware they behave this way. They are not acting maliciously but ignorantly. This fact often makes it harder for people to identify this behavior in themselves. I recently spoke with a woman who could not understand why her children had quit coming to see her. They will barely answer a phone call from her. As we spoke, I realized that she had spent most of her children's lives demanding they meet her needs. This person struggles with depression from a self-inflicted wound. Instead of repenting, she clings to that co-dependency, which, in turn, strengthens the depression. We must understand and realize that co-dependency is addictive. We get addicted to the chemical release produced by those emotions, as with anything else.

Being Zealously Affected

There is another danger associated with faulty expectations and co-dependency. In our attempt to seek solace from others, we can fall victim to similar behaviors from another person. Remember, our heart will influence our environment, drawing people with similar motives. In this peril, our heart can attract individuals who are malicious in their intent. Galatians 4:17 says, *"They zealously affect you, but not well; yea, they would exclude you, that ye might affect them."* One translation says: *"They are so concerned about you, though not with good intentions. Rather, they want to shut you out so that you would run after them."* (CEB) When someone with co-dependent inclinations is excluded from the lives of individuals whom they have deemed significant and valuable, they will inevitably pursue them to appease that sense of loss. There are malicious individuals who will exploit this vulnerability to bolster their own sense of self-importance and gain control over others. The danger of being involved in this narcissistic behavior is that it will impact your outlook.

Your mind and emotions will fall into the trap of thinking something is wrong with you or that you have done something wrong. The person excluding you will affirm those thoughts to maintain control over you. The degree to which you value that person and their place in your life determines the extent of control that person will have over you. This doesn't mean we should not value others; it simply means we need to adjust the application of value and the extent of influence others have in our lives.

Changing The Source

If we identify this behavior in ourselves, even to the tiniest degree, we must recalibrate our expectations. If we do not recalibrate, we will create and experience hurt over and over; a never-ending cycle. To recalibrate, we must change our source of acceptance. Our source of acceptance must be from God. We see this in John 2:22-25 regarding Jesus where it says, *"Now when he was in Jerusalem at the passover, in the feast day, many believed in his name, when they saw the miracles which he did. But Jesus did not **commit** himself unto them, because he knew all men, And needed not that any should testify of man: for he knew what was in man."* The word 'commit' means to entrust. It is translated that way in some Bible translations. It is a form of the Greek word for faith.[2] What this is saying is that Jesus did not put the expectations of acceptance onto others. If Jesus did what He did while He was on the earth based on others' acceptance, He would not have accomplished His work.

Jesus put His faith in God as His source, even to the death. 1 Peter 2:23 says this about Jesus on the cross: *"While being reviled and insulted, He did not revile or insult in return; while suffering, He made no threats [of vengeance], but kept **entrusting** Himself to Him who judges fairly."* (AMPC) Trusting in other humans for validation and affirmation will never work. There is too much inconsistency and instability in us; people are subject to change. On top of that, we are not designed to be the source of acceptance for each other. We can contribute to others, but we cannot be that source. Jesus knew this about humans. He knew even His disciples would let Him down and even betray Him.[3] He committed Himself to God and His word, because He knew that God never changes:

*Malachi 3:6 For I am the Lord, I **change not**; therefore ye sons of Jacob are not consumed.*

*James 1:17 Every good gift and every perfect gift is from above and comes down from the Father of lights, with whom is **no change** or shadow of turning.* (MEV)

In the same way, we must entrust ourselves to God and what He says. It is not in God's nature to change. That is why we can find peace and assurance in Him even amid other people's issues. Our emotions and minds find stability when we discover our place, identity, and acceptance in God.

Ephesians 1:6 To the praise of the glory of his grace, wherein he hath made us accepted in the beloved.

Removing faulty expectations from others brings freedom!

Chapter 10
Sticks and Stones

———•◇◇◇•———

There is an old saying that we used as children: "Sticks and stones may break my bones, but words will never hurt me." While the premise may be noble, the reality is a lie. Words can and do hurt us. This is especially true when coming from someone in authority or someone who plays a significant role in our lives, such as a parent, friend, or spouse. Words can haunt us. Like mental movies, we play back things that have been said to us. These are usually triggered by associative memory, again, like mental movies. When we focus on hurtful things that have been said to us and replay them in our minds, we are being controlled by those words. Those words begin to create the things spoken. If someone calls us worthless, and we focus on that, we will begin to incorporate those words into our belief system. Eventually, we will repeat the same words with our own mouths. We will then begin to experience what we are thinking and speaking. Our thoughts and words create our world and the perspective or perception of that world. Jesus said it like this in Matthew 12:37: *"For by thy words thou shalt be justified, and by thy words thou shalt be condemned."*

Our thoughts and words are connected: thoughts are unspoken words, and words are spoken thoughts. You will inevitably speak what you think. Thoughts are powerful enough all by themselves. However, when you speak that thought, you have empowered it to create. Hebrews 11:3 says, *"Through faith we understand that the worlds were framed by the word of God, so that things which are seen were not made of things which do appear."* God spoke His word to create what we see around us. We are created in the image of God.[1] The principle here is that, as God

61

creates by speaking, we also create by speaking. In our case, we do not create physical things as God does, bringing something from nothing. Instead, we manifest around us what we are experiencing on the inside of us. 2 Corinthians 4:13 says it like this: *"We having the same spirit of faith, according as it is written, I believed, and therefore have I spoken; we also believe, and therefore speak."* We will speak what we believe. Words carry more power than thoughts; thoughts carry the design, and words build the house.

It is almost always what other people say to and about us that influences how we think about ourselves. Behavior is learned; a child does not know danger unless an adult instructs them, and they do not know right or wrong without instruction. It is a paradox: we only become self-aware through the input of others. As we grow older and more aware, we must determine which words are true and which words are not. We also must learn the difference between condemning words of negativity and words of constructive criticism. I spoke about this in another chapter. We cannot assume that people have the same motives and intent in their words towards us. In dealing with depression, we must ask, how have words influenced me? Whose words do I hear? Whose words do I need to hear? It is imperative for our mental health that we realize the impact that words have on us. It is also imperative that we recognize when others' words towards us have become our own.

Accuser of The Brethren

We not only have to deal with others' words and our own words. We also have an adversary who wants to keep us in a place of defeat. 1 Peter 5:8 says, *"Be sober, be vigilant; because your adversary the devil, as a roaring lion, walketh about, seeking whom he may devour."* The devil, or satan, wants to devour you. How does he do that? Revelation 12:9-10 calls him the 'accuser of the brethren.'[2] That is how he tries to devour: through words of accusation. I think we have all heard things in our minds like, "A good Christian would not do that," or "How can God love you after that?". He casts doubt into our thoughts about God's love towards us, our salvation, and the truth of God's word. We see this tactic in Genesis Chapter Three in the account of the fall of man, or original (Adam's) sin. He **spoke** doubt about God and their identity.[3] Any words that tell you that God does not love you or cause you to doubt His word are from your adversary.

Speak The Word

How do we overcome words from others and from the adversary? We speak God's word. It is part of renewing the mind. We will replace words that would bring hurt to us with words of healing and faith. Revelation 12:11 says this about overcoming satan, *"And they **overcame** him by the blood of the Lamb, and by the **word** of their testimony; and they loved not their lives unto the death."* We overcome by the **word** of our testimony. What is the word of our testimony? Our testimony is that the blood of Jesus bought us back from death. His blood redeemed us! His blood makes us right with God![4] This is how we overcome any damaging words. We speak God's word. Remember the word 'meditate' we talked about previously? It means to ponder and to speak. Remember that thoughts and words are connected; we will say what we think. When we ponder on God's word, we will speak it. The repetition of this will replace words that have damaged us with words that will heal us.

Isaiah 54:17 says, *"No weapon that is formed against thee shall prosper; and every tongue* (word) *that shall rise against thee in judgment thou shalt **condemn**. This is the heritage of the servants of the LORD, and their righteousness is of me, saith the LORD."* We are to condemn any word that comes against us. Notice that it is every word that comes against us in **judgment**. The Hebrew word means 'to make a decision against you and sentence you.'[5] Those words are meant to imprison you. Those are the words that you condemn. How do we condemn those words? We speak the word of God! If a word comes to you that says you are not worth anything, then you say: "I am the pearl of great price" (Matthew 13:45-46). "I am a sweet fragrance to the Lord" (2 Corinthians 2:15). "I am the head, not the tail" (Deuteronomy 28:13).

Over and over, you counter condemning words and thoughts with what God says. I want to encourage you to get a book or devotional tool that will help you with this, as I mentioned earlier. The same process is used for fear, anxiety, doubt, etc.

Word of Caution

Speaking the word is not an exercise in positive thinking. Positive thinking is humanistic, based on human vanity. Speaking the word is saying what God says. Positive thinking is centered on you, while speaking God's word is rooted in Him. The root of all depression is its focus on self; "I'm this," or "I'm that," or "I will never be_____." The attention is on what we do, what we do not do, or what we do not have. Positive thinking is a deception, a delusion. In our own strength, no one is anything; we are all nothing. Then Jesus comes along. We see this very clearly in Ephesians Chapter Two. We were in darkness and disobedience, blinded, strangers to God, and alienated from Him. Then, Paul says in verse 13: "But now....in Christ...." We are in the light. We are reconciled. We have peace with God. The distinction is clear: without Jesus and without the word, there is no hope. That is why I focus on speaking the word. It turns our minds from us and directs them toward God. The second foundation of faith listed in Hebrews 6:1-2 is faith towards God. The first is repentance from dead works. See the distinction? I am going to repent of focusing on myself and what I do or do not do and turn my focus to God and what He has done for me in Jesus. That is the gospel, and it is our only hope.

Another word of caution I would give is in identifying words. We want to condemn words that would hurt us, not words of wisdom and correction that will help you. You must be clear in this; if you do not discern the difference between words of judgment and words of wisdom, your mind, influenced by depression, will treat all words equally. They are not equal. One leads to life; the other brings death and sorrow. How do we tell the difference? Any word that tries to convince you that you are the opposite of what God says about you is a word of judgment. Any word that leads you back to the path of what God says about you is a word of wisdom and correction. Proverbs 15:32 says, *"Those who disregard discipline despise themselves, but the one who heeds correction gains understanding."* (NIV) A word of correction will never try to convince you that you are not who God says you are. On the contrary, corrective words will lead you to the path where your life reflects what God says. I have seen people rebuke correction from the Lord, thinking that they were condemning words of judgment. Correction is not judgment. One way to discern whom you can listen to is this: follow the fruit.[6]

When I say to "follow the fruit", I mean you should listen to people with proven track records of stability and integrity. Hebrews 6:12 says that we should be *"followers of them who through faith and patience inherit the promises."* 1 Peter 5:5 says that the *"younger should submit yourselves unto the elder".* You can also say it like this: "Listen to those who have more experience and maturity than you. Observe their lives and imitate them." When someone with a proven track record of maturity and stability speaks to you, those are words you can trust. It may not be what you want to hear, but it will produce good things in your life if you take heed to them. Hebrews 13:17 says it like this: *"Remember your leaders, who spoke the word of God to you. **Consider the outcome of their way of life and imitate their faith.**"* (NIV) On the opposite side, be wary of those who do not have solid track records. If their own lives are a mess, you know not to listen to them. There is a famous quote from Otto von Bismarck that says, "Only a fool learns from his own mistakes. The wise man learns from the mistakes of others." I would add this to that quote: learn from their mistakes from a distance.

It is much better to hear a rebuke than to suffer consequences. Proverbs 17:10 says, *"A reproof enters deeper into a wise man than a hundred stripes into a fool."* Being wise is learning from those who have proven wisdom. I love what Proverbs 21:11 says on this matter: *"When a mocker is punished, the simple gain wisdom; **by paying attention to the wise they get knowledge"*** You can learn from others' mistakes, but finding trustworthy people to follow is the better path.

Words have the power to destroy and the power to heal!

Which words will you choose?

Chapter 11
Escaping Judgment

———•◇◇◇•———

One of the traps we fall into that contributes to depression is focusing on other people's behavior towards us. When we focus on how others behave towards us, we inevitably end up assigning motives to their behavior. In other words, we determine the **why** behind their actions. The scripture calls this 'judgment'. The Greek word typically used for this type of judgment is *krino*.[1] It carries with it the concept of calling into question or pronouncing an opinion. What are we calling into question? The motive behind other people's actions! We are in judgment when we pronounce an opinion about other people's motives. We become obsessed with things like: "Why did they say or do that?" or "They did this because_____." Those are statements that lead to judgment. Judgment becomes our own personal prison. Jesus said it like this in Matthew 7:1-2: *"Judge not, that ye be not judged. For with what judgment ye judge, ye shall be judged: and with what measure ye mete, it shall be measured to you again."*

Obsessing over other people's behavior puts us into that pattern of circular health. In this case, it is circular emotions. Every judgment we give comes back to us or is measured back to us because each time we think about that judgment, it is strengthened. We then begin to relate to those people we have put in judgment through that very judgment. They will, in turn, reciprocate. We create that reciprocation, but we see it as validation of our judgment. It is confirmation bias that we talked about in another chapter. We tend to focus on the things that confirm our way of thinking. We then internalize and personalize both their behavior and the validation. We think they act that way because of **us**. Judgment is a result of our perception and limits the information we can see. Breaking free from this requires changing our perception. Do not see people's actions as personal. See the truth without personalizing it. Focus on what you know about the situation; stick with the facts.

Here is a scenario: someone you know quite well walks past you without speaking. What do you know about that situation? They walked past you without speaking. That is all. If you personalize it, you will say something like, "They didn't speak to me. They must be mad at me. I must have done something to them." But what is the truth? What do you know? They walked past you without speaking. Maybe they had something else on their mind. More times than not, what people do has nothing to do with us. Here is a thought: if you believe someone is mad at you, or you want to understand their actions in any given situation, then ask them. Do not get caught up in a game of vain imaginations. Vain imaginations are where we run through different scenarios that will probably never happen. Have you ever had an argument with someone in your mind? I have a person very close to me that I catch doing that. They will say to me, "So and so might say this, but I said….." On one occasion, this person said this to me, and I pointed out that the conversation had not even happened. But they were responding as if it had already happened. In their mind, it had already happened!

In my own life, I was trapped in judgment. I was so insecure that I thought everyone's actions were against me. I am the oldest of three children, and higher expectations were placed on me than on my brother and sister because I am the oldest. My father was the type to point out the worst in me, and there was a lot of verbal abuse. I was told I would never amount to anything. When I couldn't do things I had never been taught to do, I was told I was stupid and worthless. For years, I couldn't understand why he behaved that way. The harder I tried, the worse it got. I personalized it and placed judgment on him, believing what he said. On my 30th birthday, I was extremely depressed. I prayed and asked God why my father treated me that way. The answer the Lord gave me was this: my father did not do anything **to** me; it was not personal. I was just in the way of his pain. It had nothing to do with me!

This judgment towards my father caused me to play mental movies, reinforcing my negative perception of myself. It led me to view everyone and every situation through that lens. The law of associative memory kept me in that place. If we are to break free from judgment of others, we must remember that people are dealing with their own issues, and it has nothing to do with us. Romans 14:1 in *The Message* says we all have our own history to deal with, and we should treat others gently.[2]

Projection

Placing judgment on others can come from a place of projection. Projection is where we put or project our motives onto other people's motives. It is not always the case, but it happens frequently. We assign to others the motive we would have in that same situation. For example, a person who is not outwardly affectionate may look at someone who is outwardly affectionate and think they are 'coming on' to others of the opposite sex. That may not be the truth at all. The person who is not outwardly affectionate only shows affection as a signal to their spouse for intimacy. Due to that, the tendency is to place judgment on the person who is outwardly affectionate through projection. We cannot assume that other people's motives are our motives in any given scenario. In any given scenario where the urge to judge rises in your thinking, ask yourself, "Am I projecting my own motives into this situation?"

What Is Wrong With Me?

In the last chapter, I stated that the root of all depression lies in the fact that we focus on ourselves. This is true with placing others in judgment as well. When we personalize other people's behavior towards us, what we are really doing is telling ourselves that people treat us a certain way because there is something wrong with us. When we begin to ask the question, "What is wrong with me?" we start the process of judgment towards ourselves. There is a positive Biblical judgment. We see it in 1 Corinthians 11:31: *"For if we would judge ourselves, we should not be judged."* The Greek word for 'judge' in this instance is *diakrino*.[3] It means 'to distinguish, discern'. The context of 1 Corinthians 11 is the Lord's supper, communion. It is about judging ourselves in Him; looking at what He did for us. That is the positive application of Biblical judgment. The negative application is when we judge ourselves as unworthy, which is addressed in 1 Corinthians 11:27.[4] Of course, we should be honest about our weaknesses and desire to improve in those areas. We just cannot dwell and focus on just those areas.

Along with the issue of 'what is wrong with me' is the tendency to worry about what others think of us. Of course, we want others to think well of us, and we should strive to treat people in a way that promotes that. We just cannot obsess over it. I heard this saying from one of my mentors years ago when he was describing our tendency to worry about what others think: "You are not who you think you are. You are not who others think you are. You are who you think others think you are." In other words, we will behave in a way that aligns with how we **think** others think about us. The folly in this is we do not know what others think about us. Trying to determine that is another way of placing judgment on others. Nearly every time we will think that others think badly about us. True or not, we will lean towards negativity. Focusing on that long enough will lead us down that path to depression and reinforce it. Keep this in mind when dealing with this: let your value come from God rather than men. God does not change; people do.

What others do is not personal! Let your praise be of God, not men!

70

Chapter 12
Captive Thoughts

————————•◇◇◇•————————

The key to overcoming depression is to reign in your mind. You may not have consciously chosen the situation you are in, but you are choosing to remain in your situation by continuing destructive thoughts. I have heard folks say to me, "I can't help it! I can't stop my thoughts!" We have already established the scientific principle of neuroplasticity, or brain healing. We have established the biblical principle of renewing the mind and recovering sight. It absolutely can be done. When we say we cannot stop or change, what we are really saying is, "I choose not to change." We are, in effect, saying that God's word is wrong, that God is a liar. The first part of Romans 3:4 says this: *"God forbid: yea, let God be true, but every man a liar."* We started this journey with this principle: God's word is truth. God's word says we **can** get hold of our thoughts. 2 Corinthians 10:3-5 *"For though we walk in the flesh, we do not war after the flesh:(For the weapons of our warfare are not carnal, but mighty through God to the pulling down of strong holds;) Casting down imaginations, and every high thing that exalteth itself against the knowledge of God and bringing into captivity every thought to the obedience of Christ."*

This passage of scripture tells us we do not overcome strongholds through the flesh, or by force. It finishes by telling us how to fight: we cast down our imaginations and bring our thoughts captive to the obedience of Christ. In other words, we do not focus on ourselves but on Jesus. Hebrews 12:1-2 says, *"Wherefore seeing we also are compassed about with so great a cloud of witnesses, let us lay aside every weight, and the sin which doth so easily beset us, and let us run with patience the race that is set before us,* **looking unto Jesus** *the author and finisher of our faith; who for the joy* *that was set before him endured the cross, despising the shame, and is set down at the right hand of the throne of God."* Our thoughts are the weight and causes the sin (behavior) that besets us. 'Besets' simply means entangles. We become entangled, or trapped, by our thoughts. How do we take captive our thoughts? By looking unto Jesus and His obedience in enduring the cross. We change our focus from us to Him.

The Principle of Magnification

The Biblical word for focus is 'magnify'. When we magnify something, it means we are focusing on it. When you place something under a magnifying glass, it appears bigger. When we magnify things in our minds, those things appear bigger to us. That is why we get overwhelmed. Our perception is that of magnification. Remember this about perception: there is a difference between the way we feel and think the world is, and the way it really is. What we magnify is what we experience. As with every principle we have seen so far, that holds true both positively and negatively. If we magnify the problem, we experience more of the problem in our emotions. If we magnify the solution (God), we experience more of the solution in our emotions. In the context of taking our thoughts captive, we must choose to magnify God and His word. Psalm 34:3 *"O **magnify** the Lord with me, and let us exalt his name together."* When we do this, we have a promise from the Lord that we will have peace. Isaiah 26:3 says, *"Thou wilt keep him in perfect peace, whose mind is **stayed** on thee: because he trusteth in thee."* That is His promise to us.

The Fruit of Our Lips

One aspect of magnifying the Lord and taking our thoughts captive is to hear our own voices magnifying God. Our words are part of the problem in getting us into depression, and they also play a part in the solution and getting us free. If you speak about the problem, then you must also speak about the solution. Hebrews 13:15 says, *"By him therefore let us offer the sacrifice of praise to God* **continually**, *that is, the fruit of our lips giving thanks to his name."* Regardless of feelings, praise Him and magnify Him! Your quality of life depends on it. If you do not know what to say, then play worship songs and sing along. You might feel foolish at first. But, cast down that imagination and high thing that would exalt itself against the knowledge of magnifying Him and do it anyway! Praise opens prison doors! In Acts 16, we see Paul and Silas thrown in jail for casting an evil spirit out of a woman. There were men who were making money from the divination she did through the evil spirit, and they had Paul and Silas arrested.

While in jail, we see them do this is verses 25-26: *"And at midnight Paul and Silas prayed, and sang praises unto God: and the prisoners heard them. And suddenly there was a great earthquake, so that the foundations of the prison were shaken: and immediately all the doors were opened, and every one's bands were loosed."* Magnifying God and looking unto Jesus will help us take our thoughts captive. Our prison doors will open, and our shackles will fall off!

God wants to break down your prison doors and break your shackles!

Chapter 13
Dignity and Worth

————•◇◇◇•————

While many things contribute to depression, ultimately, depression is an inside job. Whether it is perception, projection, judgment, or anything else we have discussed, those are symptoms rather than causes. The root cause of all depression is a negative, unhealthy inward focus. It is a form of narcissism. While the basic definition of narcissism is 'an excessive admiration for oneself'[1], I would suggest that even a negative, obsessive focus on oneself is narcissistic in nature; the focus is still on myself and how things affect me. The Bible describes it as 'seeking their own righteousness' in Romans 10:3.[2] We call it self-righteousness in Christian terminology. When people hear the term 'self-righteous,' it generally conjures the image of someone bragging to others about how good they are while at the same time belittling others who do not quite 'make the grade.' Jesus tells a parable about this specifically:

*Luke 18:9-12 "He told this parable to some who **trusted in themselves, as though they were righteous, and despised others**: "Two men went up to the temple to pray, the one a Pharisee and the other a tax collector. The Pharisee stood and prayed these things about himself, 'God, I thank You that I am not like other men: extortioners, unjust, adulterers, or even like this tax collector. I fast twice a week, and I tithe of all that I earn'." (MEV)*

Though the tendency is to see self-righteousness in this way, the truth is that righteousness is on a spectrum. At the top, there is arrogance and self-importance. At the bottom, there is anxiety and depression. They are both results of self-righteousness, or narcissism; an obsessive focus on self. The Apostle Paul wrote about it in Romans 10:6-7: *"But the righteousness which is of faith speaketh on this wise, Say not in thine heart, Who shall ascend into heaven? (that is, to bring Christ down from above:) Or, Who shall descend into the deep? (that is, to bring up Christ again from the dead.)"* You cannot go high enough (arrogance), and you cannot go low enough (depression). The root of all obsessive self-focus comes down to not having a sense of worth. More specifically, it is trying to gain a sense of worth from within ourselves; trusting in ourselves that we are, or can be, righteous (worthy). The Old Testament law and the traditions of religion prove that we are not, nor can we become, worthy on our own. The more we rely on ourselves, the more we are disposed to being arrogant or depressed.

Our worth must come from something greater than ourselves. As believers, our worth must come from what Jesus did for us: becoming the substitution for us and bearing the judgment of sin. That is what the Apostle Paul is speaking about in Romans 10:6-7 above. We see something similar in Ephesians 4:10: *"He that descended is the same also that ascended up far above all heavens, that he might fill all things."* We turn our attention to Jesus, the author, and finisher of our faith. (Hebrews 12:2) We take our thoughts captive to His obedience! His obedience filled all things. I hear believers and ministers use this term: self-worth. Self-worth is what causes our problems in the first place. We should be looking for Christ-worth. God created us with dignity and worth. We see this clearly in Hebrews 2:6-7: *"But one in a certain place testified, saying, What is man, that thou art mindful of him? or the son of man that thou visitest him? Thou madest him a little lower than the angels; thou crownedst him with glory and honour, and didst set him over the works of thy hands:"*

The words 'glory and honor' mean dignity (value) and worth in Greek.[3] God created us to operate in this world with a sense of value from being created by him. This passage in Hebrews shows us how much value He places on us: He set us over the works of His hands, or His creation. He valued us enough to place us in dominion over the earth.[4] Something to point out here is the phrase 'made him (man) a little lower than the angels.' The author of Hebrews is quoting Psalm 8:3-6. In that psalm, the word 'angels' is the Hebrew word Elohim, which means gods or godhead.[5] The psalmist is saying that God created us just a little lower than God, or the Trinity: Father, Son, and Holy Spirit. That is where we get our worth: from God! God created Adam and Eve with dignity and worth. When Adam sinned, he lost that sense of dignity and worth. He lost confidence before God. We see this in Genesis 3:7-8: after they ate of the tree of the knowledge of good and evil, they covered themselves and hid from God.[6] If they had not lost that sense of dignity and worth, they would have had no need to hide from God.

Jesus restored our sense of dignity and worth. Romans 10:11 and 1 Peter 2:6 specifically say that if we believe in Him (Jesus), we will not be put to shame (lose our dignity and worth).[7] That is why it is so important to renew our minds to the finished work of Jesus. In and of ourselves, we will never be able to find dignity and worth. We will constantly be trying to find it through our achievements or through others. We are created to find dignity and worth through fellowship with God, which only comes through Christ Jesus.

Faith Righteousness

At the very heart of the New Testament is a concept called *faith righteousness*. This concept is simple: we cannot be righteous on our own and must trust God for righteousness. Righteous simply means a sense of rightness, a right standing with God. God provided righteousness to us in Jesus on the cross. 2 Corinthians 5:21 says, *"God made Him (Jesus) who knew no sin to be sin for us, that we might become the righteousness of God in Him."* That is why the author of Hebrews named these as the first two foundations of faith in Hebrews 6:1-2: repentance from dead works and faith towards God. Without these foundations, we will always struggle with a sense of worth. A dead work is anything we do to make ourselves righteous or worthy, either to the top of the spectrum or to the bottom of the spectrum. It is faith in our own ability, trusting ourselves. We become arrogant to hide where we fall short, and we become depressed when we realize our own failings. Neither of these is faith towards God. Faith towards God is this:

Romans 10:6-7 "But the righteousness which is based on faith says, "Do not say in your heart, 'Who will ascend into heaven?' (that is, to bring Christ down), or, 'Who will descend into the deep?'(that is, to bring Christ up from the dead)."

We saw this passage in the previous section of this chapter. In this context, faith righteousness teaches us that what Jesus did took care of all our needs for righteousness. We cannot go higher than Him, and we cannot go lower than Him. We cannot trust in our talents, riches, intellect, or appearance for righteousness. We cannot trust in punishing ourselves, feeling bad enough long enough, or doing good deeds for righteousness. Understanding that righteousness is a work of God through the Lord Jesus shows us the immense value God has for us. In fact, when we do not realize this, we are in sin. The second half of Romans 14:23 says, *"for whatsoever is not of faith is sin."* If righteousness is of faith, but we are trying to go high or low for it, then we are in sin. We are operating in dead works: not trusting God but ourselves. We should not be condemned when we realize that, but we should repent from dead works. God will help you with that. Dead works are why we stay in our bad thinking. It comes back to the principle of 'circular health,' only spiritually in this case.

When we grasp hold of faith righteousness, it will bring peace to our minds. Consider Romans 5:1, *"Therefore being justified by faith, we have peace with God through our Lord Jesus Christ:"* The word 'justified' simply means *made righteous.*[9] Because He has made us righteous, we now have peace with God. That peace can also affect your mind and your thoughts. We have no worth apart from Jesus. But in Him, we have everything. *Acts 17:28 "For in him we live, and move, and have our being; as certain also of your own poets have said, For we are also his offspring."*

Acknowledging Every Good Thing

As we have seen throughout this journey, replacing your thoughts is of the utmost importance. One of the hardest thoughts to replace for someone struggling with depression are negative thoughts about oneself. However, we must say what God says about anything or situation. Philemon 6 says, *"That the communication of thy faith may become effectual by the acknowledging of every good thing which is in you in Christ Jesus."* Our faith will only be effective as we acknowledge **every good thing** that is in us. The qualifying factor here is 'in Christ Jesus'. We covered that in the last section: we have no worth, or inheritance, apart from Jesus. Philemon says that we are not to just **know** every good thing; we are to **acknowledge** every good thing. We think about it; we speak it, and then we share it (the communication of our faith). It is hard to see in ourselves what God sees in us. But see it, and acknowledge it, we must. We do that through Biblical meditation and confession. This is where a good workbook would help organize scriptures for you. The more you do this, the more your thinking changes. That, in turn, changes your behavior, which changes your beliefs. Eventually, your cycle of circular health changes towards what God has for you; your faith will become effective, and you will walk the paths of righteousness[10] God has for you.

The Lord is my shepherd! I shall not want!

Chapter 14
Trusting God

———————•◇◇•———————

Ultimately, to overcome anything, we must come to a place of faith towards God. We have established that we cannot look to ourselves to find the solutions for our freedom. Looking to ourselves is what produced our mess to begin with. It is foolish to think that since we produced the problem, then we can fix the problem alone. Jesus called this a house divided.[1] Others can help, but applying principles of the word of God brings wholeness. Coming to a place of faith in any area, including depression, means we must be able to trust God and what He says in His word. The application of faith rests on trusting God's character. If you cannot trust God's motive and intent towards you, you will not trust what He says. All of faith hinges on God's character; more specifically, it hinges on your belief in God's character, who He is. Will you believe who God says He is, and who He has revealed Himself to be through His word? Or will you believe what tradition and religion have told people about God? We started this journey with the premise that God's word is absolute truth. We do not have the space here to do an exhaustive study of God's nature and character. But we can look at enough to help faith come alive.

The first thing we must see about God is this: He is for you and not against you! Romans 8:31-32 says, *"What shall we then say to these things? If God be for us, who can be against us? He that spared not his own Son, but delivered him up for us all, how shall he not with him also freely give us all things?"* This passage of scripture lays it out plainly: God is for you! He does not want you to suffer in depression. He wants good for you. Religion and tradition will tell you God brings things upon you to test you; that in His mysterious ways He causes calamity, sickness, and chaos to bring about good. But consider James 1:13: *"Let no man say when he is tempted, I am tempted of God: for God cannot be tempted with **evil**, neither tempteth he any man:"* In Greek, the root word for 'evil' means *with malice.*[2] The word itself means *troublesome, injurious, destructive.* This verse says God does **not** tempt us from a place of malice to bring trouble, injury, or destruction. James 1:17 says, *"Every good gift and every perfect gift is from above, and cometh down from the Father of lights, with whom is no variableness, neither shadow of turning."* God is light, and there is no darkness (malice, evil) in Him.

The word 'tempts' in James 1:13 means to test, try, or scrutinize (looking to find fault)[3]. He does not work evil to bring good. God works good from evil. Since God is for you, then all His principles and instructions in His word are there to help you be free, not to bind you up.

*Hebrews 4:16 "Let us therefore come boldly unto the throne of grace, that we may obtain **mercy**, and find **grace** to **help** in time of need."*

*Hebrews 13:6 "So that we may boldly say, **The Lord is my helper**, and I will not fear what man shall do unto me."*

The Goodness and Love of God

Since God desires good for us, then we must conclude that He is good. This is how He has revealed Himself in the scriptures:

*Exodus 34:6 "And the Lord passed by before him, and proclaimed, The Lord, The Lord God, merciful and gracious, longsuffering, and **abundant in goodness** and truth,"*

*Psalm 34:8 "O taste and see that **the Lord is good**: blessed is the man that trusteth in him."*

In Psalm 34:8, the psalmist ties the Lord's goodness to trusting Him. Trusting Him begins with believing that He is good. If we cannot believe He is good, then we cannot believe He wants good for us and will help us. The struggle mankind has had through the centuries is this very thing: the goodness of God. Yet, our faith hinges on this one thing. There are so many scriptures that talk about God's goodness. I encourage you to simply do a Google search on scriptures on the goodness of God. It is a major defining characteristic of His nature.

Tied to the concept of God's goodness is His love. This is another area in which mankind has struggled. When experiencing depression, it is hard to believe that God loves us. The very nature of depression causes us to think we are unlovable. The more we try to experience love from a place of thinking we are unlovable, the more we will experience a sense of rejection or judgment. We will mistakenly think that the rejection we feel is from God. It is simply an issue of perception. Perception is how we think something is, but it is rarely the truth of how something is. Again, the word of God is our standard of truth, and it says this in 1 John 4:16: *"And we have known and* **believed the love that God hath to us. God is love;** *and he that dwelleth in love dwelleth in God, and God in him."* God **is** love! 2 Corinthians 13 is the famous 'love' chapter of the Bible. Read what love is from that chapter, and that is who God is. Romans 8:38-39 says, *"For I am persuaded, that neither death, nor life, nor angels, nor principalities, nor powers, nor things present, nor things to come, Nor height, nor depth, nor any other creature, shall be able to separate us from the* **love of God**, *which is in Christ Jesus our Lord."*

Coming to a place of faith in God's love will bring comfort to our hearts. If nothing can separate us from God's love, then we can have the confidence to come before Him. Jesus calls the Holy Spirit the Comforter.[4] He is also called the Spirit of Truth[5], but He always brings truth with comfort. Why? It is His nature. He is full of goodness and love! We can trust Him. He is holy, which means He is pure. Being pure means He has no ill intent or motives of malice. He will bring correction to His children[6], but it will always be from a place of comfort and love. Breaking free from depression will require correction. I love how my pastor says it, "Correction is direction, not rejection." Correction from love will never bring fear. God does not want you to fear Him but to worship and reverence Him. Fear does not work the purposes of God. It was fear that caused Adam and Eve to hide from God. As with the goodness of God, I encourage you to do a simple Google search on all the scriptures that say, 'fear not.' 1 John 4:18 says, *"There is no fear in love; but perfect love casteth out fear: because fear hath torment. He that feareth is not made perfect in love."*

At its core, depression is a form of fear. Being established in God's love will drive out fear. It will cause you to stand and allow the word of God to become effective in your heart. Galatians 5:6 tells us that faith works by love. Becoming convinced of God's goodness and love is the beginning of faith; it is the foundation where faith towards God can grow.

God is for you!
He is good and loves you!

Chapter 15
Accepted In The Beloved

———•◇◇◇•———

Depression carries with it the belief that we are not worthy of others' acceptance. We carry that belief over to God as well. As I said at the beginning of the last chapter, we must come to a place of trusting God. With that in mind, what does the word of God say about this belief? When it comes to God's acceptance, the scripture is very clear. Ephesians 1:6 says, *"To the praise of the glory of his grace, wherein he hath made us **accepted in the beloved**."* We are accepted by God in the Lord Jesus. I said this before, but it bears repeating: we cannot focus on ourselves but on who we are in Christ. Remember Hebrews 12:2: *"looking unto Jesus, the author and finisher of our faith."* We are the problem; He is the solution. If we base our acceptance on what we do, we will fail miserably. If we base our acceptance on other people, we will always be let down. People are not stable. They shift like the wind. We must build on the one thing in this universe that is unchanging and constant: the love of God. Malachi 3:6 says, *"For I am the Lord, **I change not**, therefore ye sons of Jacob are not consumed."*

God does not change, and we can trust Him. If He does not change, and the Word of God says we are accepted in the beloved, then His acceptance does not change. When we are convinced of this, our sense of rejection withers away. We do not have to carry the need for others' acceptance. We can take this burden off others. When we remove that burden from others, we will find that others will accept us, whereas before, they would reject us. Placing a burden on others will create rejection. It is a spiritual law. As I stated in the last chapter, at its core, depression is fear. We fear rejection yet create that which we fear through neediness. When we fear rejection, we are telling our heart that we fear people. We may not fear them physically, but we fear them emotionally. We fear they will withhold acceptance. When God is the source of our acceptance, we remove fear from the equation. Psalm 27:1 says, *"The Lord is my light and my salvation; whom shall I fear? the Lord is the strength of my life; of whom shall I be afraid?"*

Realizing that we are accepted in the beloved removes the fear of others. Since our source is God, we do not need to fear that others will not meet those needs. They are already met in Him! Colossians 2:10 says it this way, *"And ye are complete in him, which is the head of all principality and power:"* All of our needs are met in Him. We do not need to look anywhere else, or to anyone else. Acts 17:28 says, *"For in him we live, and move, and have our being; as certain also of your own poets have said, For we are also his offspring."* The result of faith is that this scripture becomes our reality.

The Lifter of My Head

It is God's desire that we walk in a high quality of life, a holy quality of life. Jesus said in John 10:10 that He had come so that we could have an abundant life[1]. That is a New Testament promise and benefit. Under the New Testament, we are called 'the seed of Abraham' because we are in Jesus[1]. We are heirs to the promise and blessings given to Abraham. In Luke 13:10-16, we see Jesus heal a woman on the Sabbath day who was crippled for eighteen years. Her back was crooked, and she could not straighten it. The leader of the synagogue got angry with Jesus for healing her on the Sabbath. Jesus replied in verse 16, *"And ought not this woman, being a daughter of Abraham, whom Satan hath bound, lo, these eighteen years, be loosed from this bond on the sabbath day?"* Jesus was saying that being a descendant of Abraham, Abraham's seed, gave her the right to be healed. But notice this: if her back was crooked, her head was down. Jesus, by healing her, lifted her head. He did so because it was her right as Abraham's seed.

That same promise goes for us as well since we are Abraham's seed for being in Jesus. A bowed head is symbolic of someone in depression, shame, and a low sense of worth. I can remember keeping my head and eyes down for years. I would avoid eye contact with people because I felt unworthy, not good enough. I assumed people saw me the same way that I saw myself. I remember walking through a store with my wife, and she told me to get my head up and walk straight. I can remember reading this scripture: *Psalm 3:3 "But thou, O Lord, art a shield for me; my glory, and the lifter up of mine head."* Not only do we have a right to walk in dignity and worth as the seed of Abraham, but God's character is the lifter of our head. He desires that for us. This is not to be confused with arrogance. It is humility; knowing that without Him we are nothing. But at the same time not shying away from His word, His promises, and His blessings.

Jesus bore our shame so He could be the lifter of our heads. In Hebrews 12:2 we see, *"Looking unto Jesus the author and finisher of our faith; who for the joy that was set before him endured the cross, **despising the shame**, and is set down at the right hand of the throne of God."* He endured shame on the cross. When Jesus died, John 19:30 says, *"When Jesus therefore had received the vinegar, he said, It is finished: and **he bowed his head**, and gave up the ghost."* He bowed His head; He endured our shame. Everything He endured on the cross was to pay for us, to redeem us. We do not have to walk with our heads bowed, literally or figuratively. It has been paid!

Hope Restored

When battling depression, we lose sight of hope. The Greek definition for 'hope' is a confident expectation of good.[3] We quit expecting good because we do not think we deserve it, that we are unworthy. As we have seen, God is good and wants good for us. He wants to restore hope to us. In Luke 4:18-19, Jesus says, *"The Spirit of the Lord is upon me, because he hath anointed me to preach the gospel to the poor; he hath sent me to heal the brokenhearted, to preach deliverance to the captives, and **recovering of sight** to the blind, to set at liberty them that are bruised, To preach the acceptable year of the Lord."* The phrase 'recovering of sight' comes from a root word that means 'restoration.' It also means 'to look up'.[4] He is the lifter of my head! It is not just physical sight He desires to restore to us. He also wants to restore spiritual sight as well. Losing sight of something means we have lost our way and cannot find the way back. Hope sees the path of our life.

From a spiritual sense, hope is the blueprint for life. When we quit hope, we quit God's plans for us. One of the many effects of depression is that it robs us of vision and purpose. The first part of Proverbs 29:18 says, *"Where there is no vision, the people perish."* The Lord wants to put you back on the path that you left when depression took over. He does not change His mind about your purpose![5] But to get there, we must do what Romans 4:18 says Abraham did: *"Who against hope believed in hope, that he might become the father of many nations, according to that which was spoken, So shall thy seed be."* Abraham **believed** in hope: the blueprint, the plan, the vision, the purpose. We cannot fulfill our purpose without hope. Restoring sight (hope) is part of Jesus' ministry to us. If you let Him, He will restore hope to you!

Beauty For Ashes

Luke 4:18-19 is part of a passage taken from an Old Testament scripture: Isaiah 61:1-3. Isaiah 61:1-3 says it like this: *"The Spirit of the Lord God is upon me; because the Lord hath anointed me to preach good tidings unto the meek; he hath sent me to bind up the brokenhearted, to proclaim liberty to the captives, and the opening of the prison to them that are bound; To proclaim the acceptable year of the Lord, and the day of vengeance of our God; to comfort all that mourn; To appoint unto them that mourn in Zion, to give unto them **beauty for ashes**, the oil of joy for mourning, the garment of praise for the spirit of heaviness; that they might be called trees of righteousness, the planting of the Lord, that he might be glorified."* 'Beauty for ashes' is a phrase that shows a life restored by God. In ancient times, when people were sorrowful or broken, they would take ashes and pour them on themselves to show their mourning. So 'beauty for ashes' is the Lord's way of saying He intends to redeem and restore us. It shows His intent towards us in that He does not want us to stay in that state of sorrow and mourning. He does not want us to live in a state of brokenness.

Remember what we saw in the first section of this chapter with Colossians 2:10: *"And ye are complete in him...."*. It is God's desire that we be complete, not broken. There is a brokenness before the Lord, but it is not a brokenness of guilt and condemnation. It is a brokenness of humbling ourselves before the Lord and allowing Him to guide our lives. It is submitting our opinions, views, and plans to His opinions, views, and plans. David said it like this in Psalm 51:17: *"The sacrifices of God are a broken spirit: a broken and a contrite heart, O God, thou wilt not despise."* When we are broken in depression or condemnation, we are living below the quality of life He wants for us. To God, it is ashes. His intent for mankind all along was for us to live in dignity and worth, or beauty. Jesus' mission was to replace our ashes with beauty. Our salvation and life in Him are our beauty.

You are accepted in the beloved!

Conclusion

————•◇◇◇•————

We are not equipped emotionally to carry guilt and shame. It is unnatural to us. That is why it creates such havoc in our minds, emotions, and bodies. God created us to be at rest from a place of value and purpose in Him. All the principles shared in this book will help you find that place of rest. These principles are how we operate the way God intended for us. I know these principles work because I have applied them in my own life. These are the same principles I applied to break free from depression. These are the same principles I use to help others. Just recently, I ministered to a person who was bedridden from anxiety, fear, and depression. This person was afraid to be alone. They had to have someone with them all the time. Within a few months, this person has become happy, active in social interaction, and doing things they were not doing a few short months ago, even spending time alone. That is the power of God's word and principles!

These are not one-time fixes. The mind must be constantly renewed. The very definition of 'renewing the mind' implies repetition. Our old nature is always waiting to take back over. Does it get easier? Yes, it does! As we renew our minds, we become established in these principles; they replace the old way of thinking and behaving. But we must always be guarding our heart. Remember Proverbs 4:23: *"Above all else, guard your heart, for everything you do flows from it."* (NIV) Once you experience freedom, you will be determined to never return to that place of darkness again. My prayer for you is that you will seek God's counsel and guidance and allow Him to work grace in your life; that you will allow Him to restore you to the place He wants for you; that you will see yourself the way He sees you; that you will have victory over depression!

Break Free!

Bibliography

Chapter 2

1.https://www.mdedge.com/neurology/epilepsyresourcecenter/article/976 03/epilepsy-seizures/how-does-depression-affect?sso=true

2.https://www.nimh.nih.gov/news/science-news/2018/inflammation-in-pregnant-moms-linked-to-childs-brain-development.shtml

3.https://www.healthline.com/health/chemical-imbalance-in-the-brain

3a.https://thehill.com/changing-america/well-being/mental-health/3569506-depression-is- likely-not-caused-by-a-chemical-imbalance-in-the-brain-study-says/

4.https://www.bridgestorecovery.com/blog/how-major-depression-affects-the-brain-and-body-why-residential-treatment-can-help/

5.https://www.nimh.nih.gov/news/science-news/2018/inflammation-in-pregnant- moms-linked-to-childs-brain-development.shtml

6.https://www.mdedge.com/neurology/epilepsyresourcecenter/article/976 03/epilepsy-seizures/how-does-depression-affect?sso=true

7.https://www.bridgestorecovery.com/blog/how-major-depression-affects-the-brain-and-body-why-residential-treatment-can-help/

8.https://pubmed.ncbi.nlm.nih.gov/31745237/

9.https://my.clevelandclinic.org/health/diseases/21521-psychosomatic-disorder

10. And so we who are born of the Holy Spirit are persecuted now by those who want us to keep the Jewish laws, just as Isaac, the child of promise, was persecuted by Ishmael, the slave-wife's son. (The Living Bible)

11. 1 Cor. 10:13 No temptation has overtaken you such as is common to man; but God *is* faithful, who will not allow you to be tempted beyond what you are able, but with the temptation will also make the way of escape, that you may be able to bear *it*. (NKJV)

Chapter 3

1. https://www.news-medical.net/health/Intrusive-Thoughts-and-Depression.aspx

2. Strong's Concordance- Strong's Number 5590: psuche Thayer's Greek-English Lexicon of the New Testament- the soul: the seat of the feelings, desires, affections, aversions

3. See the movie 'What The Bleep Do We Know?'

4. https://qbi.uq.edu.au/brain/brain-functions/what-are-neurotransmitters

5. https://www.medicalnewstoday.com/articles/326649#functions

6. https://www.ncbi.nlm.nih.gov/pmc/articles/PMC4458710

Chapter 4

1. https://www.mentalhelp.net/depression/psychology-behavioral-theories/

2. Strong's Concordance- Strong's Number 2669: kataponeō Thayer's Greek-English Lexicon of the New Testament- to tire down with toil, exhaust with labor

3. Strong's Concordance- Strong's Number 928: basanizō- to torture

4. https://www.abc.net.au/radionational/programs/allinthemind/neuroplasticity-and-how-the-brain-can-heal-itself/6406736

5. https://www.annualreviews.org/doi/abs//10.1146/annurev-neuro-072116-031204

5a. https://www.ncbi.nlm.nih.gov/pmc/articles/PMC4458710

6. Strong's Concordance- Strong's Number 3339: metamorphoo- to transform, change, transfigure

7. Strong's Concordance- Strong's Number 342: anakainosis- renovation; renewing

8. https://getpocket.com/explore/item/the-neuroscience-of-breaking-out-of-negative-thinking-and-how-to-do-it-in-under-30-seconds?utm_source=pocket-newtab

9. Matthew 4:4 But he answered and said, It is written, Man shall not live by bread alone, but by every word that proceedeth out of the mouth of God.

10. Mark 6:41 And when he had taken the five loaves and the two fishes, he looked up to heaven, and blessed, and brake the loaves, and gave them to his disciples to set before them; and the two fishes divided he among them all.

11. Strong's Concordance- Strong's Number 308: anablepo

12. Strong's Concordance- Strong's Number 3340: metanoeo

13. Strong's Concordance- Strong's Number 3341: metanoia- compunction (for guilt, including reformation); by implication, reversal (of (another's) decision)

Chapter 5

1. https://yourstory.com/2015/04/power-of-thoughts

2. Rom. 6:16 Know ye not, that to whom ye yield yourselves servants to obey, his servants ye are to whom ye obey; whether of sin unto death, or of obedience unto righteousness?

3. See Note 1 above.

4. https://www.ncbi.nlm.nih.gov/pmc/articles/PMC2802367

5. https://well.org/mindset/how-your-subconscious-mind-controls-your-behavior/

6. https://exploringyourmind.com/the-quantum-mind-transform-reality/

7. For more information and research on the heart, visit www.impactministries.com.
Dr. Jim Richards has an extensive program called 'Heart Physics'.

8. Psalm 139:14 I will praise thee; for I am fearfully and wonderfully made: marvellous are thy works; and that my soul knoweth right well.

9. Matthew 12:36 But I say unto you, That every idle word that men shall speak, they shall give account thereof in the day of judgment

10. Strong's Concordance-Strongs Number 1897: hagah

11. Matthew 7:1-2 Judge not, that ye be not judged. For with what judgment ye judge ye shall be judged: and with what measure ye mete, it shall be measured to you again.

Chapter 6

1. Strong's Concordance-Strong's Number 954: buwsh

2. Hebrews 6:1 Therefore leaving the principles of the doctrine of Christ, let us go on unto perfection; not laying again the foundation of repentance from dead works, and of faith toward God,

Hebrews 9:14 How much more shall the blood of Christ, who through the eternal Spirit offered himself without spot to God, purge your conscience from dead works to serve the living God?

3. Isaiah 64:6 But we are all as an unclean thing, and all our righteousnesses are as filthy rags; and we all do fade as a leaf; and our iniquities, like the wind, have taken us away.

Romans 10:3 For they being ignorant of God's righteousness, and going about to establish their own righteousness, have not submitted themselves unto the righteousness of God.

4. Strong's Concordance-Strong's Number 3954: parresia

Chapter 7

1. Strong's Concordance-Strong's Number 1680: elpis

2. Matthew 12:43

3. John 17:6 I have revealed you to those whom you gave me out of the world. They were yours; you gave them to me and they have obeyed your word. (NIV)

4. Genesis 22:14
a. Strongs's Concordance-Strong's Number 3070: Jehovah-jireh- the Lord will see to it, provide.

5. Strongs's Concordance-Strong's Number 4654: skotizo

6. Strongs's Concordance-Strong's Number 3154: mataioo

7. Google Dictionary-futile: incapable of producing any useful result; pointless

8. Ephesians 4:17 This I say therefore, and testify in the Lord, that ye henceforth walk not as other Gentiles walk, in the vanity of their mind,

9. 1 Crinthians 10:13 There hath no temptation taken you but such as is common to man: but God is faithful, who will not suffer you to be tempted

above that ye are able; but will with the temptation also make a way to escape, that ye may be able to bear it.

Chapter 8
1. Hebrews 12:14 Follow peace with all men, and holiness, without which no man shall see the Lord:

2. Strongs's Concordance-Strong's Number 3392: miaino

Chapter 9
1. Acts 20:29 For I know this, that after my departing shall grievous wolves enter in among you, not sparing the flock.

2. Strongs's Concordance-Strong's Number 4100: pisteuo

3. Matt. 26:34 (Peter) Jesus said unto him, Verily I say unto thee, That this night, before the cock crow, thou shalt deny me thrice.

John 13:21 (Judas) When Jesus had thus said, he was troubled in spirit, and testified, and said, Verily, verily, I say unto you, that one of you shall betray me.

Chapter 10
1. Genesis 1:26 And God said, Let us make man in our image, after our likeness: and let them have dominion over the fish of the sea, and over the fowl of the air, and over the cattle, and over all the earth, and over every creeping thing that creepeth upon the earth.

2. Revelation 12:9-10 And the great dragon was cast out, that old serpent, called the Devil, and Satan, which deceiveth the whole world: he was cast out into the earth, and his angels were cast out with him.And I heard a loud voice saying in heaven, Now is come salvation, and strength, and the kingdom of our God, and the power of his Christ: for the accuser of our brethren is cast down, which accused them before our God day and night

3. Genesis 3:1-5 Now the serpent was more subtil than any beast of the field which the Lord God had made. And he said unto the woman, Yea, hath God said, Ye shall not eat of every tree of the garden? And the woman said unto the serpent, we may eat of the fruit of the trees of the garden: But of the fruit of the tree which is in the midst of the garden, God hath said, Ye

shall not eat of it, neither shall ye touch it, lest ye die. And the serpent said unto the woman, Ye shall not surely die:: For God doth know that in the day ye eat thereof, then your eyes shall be as opened, and ye shall be as gods, knowing good and evil

4. 1 Peter 1:18-19 Forasmuch as ye know that ye were not redeemed with corruptible things, as silver and gold, from your vain conversation received by tradition from your fathers; But with the precious blood of Christ, as of a lamb without blemish and without spot

2 Corinthians 5:21 For he hath made him to be sin for us, who knew no sin; that we might be made the righteousness of God in him.

5. Strongs's Concordance-Strong's Number 4941- mishpat

6. Matthew 7:20 Wherefore by their fruits ye shall know them.

Hebrews 6:12 That ye be not slothful, but followers of them who through faith and patience inherit the promises.

Chapter 11
1. Strongs's Concordance-Strong's Number 2919

2. Romans 14:1 (TMB) Welcome with open arms fellow believers who don't see things the way you do. And don't jump all over them every time they do or say something you don't agree with—even when it seems that they are strong on opinions but weak in the faith department. Remember, they have their own history to deal with. Treat them gently.

3. Strongs's Concordance-Strong's Number 1252

4. 1 Corinthians 11:27 Wherefore whosoever shall eat this bread, and drink this cup of the Lord, unworthily, shall be guilty of the body and blood of the Lord.

Chapter 13
1. Merriam-Webster Online Dictionary: narcissistic- extremely self-centered with an exaggerated sense of self-importance : marked by or characteristic of excessive admiration of or infatuation with oneself.

2. Romans 10:3 For they being ignorant of God's righteousness, and going about to establish their own righteousness, have not submitted themselves unto the righteousness of God.

3. Glory: Strongs's Concordance-Strong's Number 1391-doxa a good opinion Thayer's Greek Lexicon: opinion, view, magnificence, dignity, grace, excellence, majesty

Honor: Strongs's Concordance-Strong's Number 5092-time (tee-may) worth, value Thayer's Greek Lexicon: a valuing, honor

4. Genesis 1:26 And God said, Let us make man in our image, after our likeness: and let them have dominion over the fish of the sea, and over the owl of the air, and over the cattle, and over all the earth, and over every creeping thing that creepeth upon the earth.

5. Strongs's Concordance-Strong's Number 430-elohim

6. Genesis 3:6-8 And when the woman saw that the tree was good for food, and that it was pleasant to the eyes, and a tree to be desired to make one wise, she took of the fruit thereof, and did eat, and gave also unto her husband with her; and he did eat. And the eyes of them both were opened, and they knew that they were naked; and they sewed fig leaves together, and made themselves aprons. And they heard the voice of the Lord God walking in the garden in the cool of the day: and Adam and his wife hid themselves from the presence of the Lord God amongst the trees of the garden.

7. Romans 10:11 For the scripture saith, Whosoever believeth on him shall not be ashamed.

1 Peter 2:6 For also it is contained in the Scripture, "Look! I lay in Zion a chief cornerstone, elect, precious and he who believes in Him shall never be put to shame." (MEV)

8. Hebrews 6:1-2 Therefore leaving the principles of the doctrine of Christ, let us go on unto perfection; not laying again the foundation of repentance from dead works, and of faith toward God, Of the doctrine of baptisms, and of laying on of hands, and of resurrection of the dead, and of eternal judgment.

9. Strongs's Concordance-Strong's Number 1344- dikaioo

10. Psalm 23:3 He restoreth my soul: he leadeth me in the paths of righteousness for his name's sake.

Chapter 14

1. Matthew 12:24-25 But when the Pharisees heard it, they said, This fellow doth not cast out devils, but by Beelzebub the prince of the devils. And Jesus knew their thoughts, and said unto them, Every kingdom divided against itself is brought to desolation; and every city or house divided against itself shall not stand.

2. Strongs's Concordance-Strong's Number 2556- kakos

3. Strongs's Concordance-Strong's Number 3985- peirazo Thayer's Greek-English Lexicon: to try, make trial of, test; to test one maliciously; to solicit to sin, to tempt; to inflict evils upon one in order to prove his character and the steadfastness of his faith:

4. John 14:26   But the Comforter, which is the Holy Ghost, whom the Father will send in my name, he shall teach you all things, and bring all things to your remembrance, whatsoever I have said unto you.

5. John 16:13 Howbeit when he, the Spirit of truth, is come, he will guide you into all truth: for he shall not speak of himself; but whatsoever he shall hear, that shall he speak: and he will shew you things to come.

6. Hebrews 12:5-7 And have you forgotten his encouraging words spoken to you as his children? He said, "My child, don't underestimate the value of the discipline and training of the Lord God, or get depressed when he has to correct you. For the Lord's training of your life is the evidence of his faithful love. And when he draws you to himself, it proves you are his delightful child." Fully embrace God's correction as part of your training, for he is doing what any loving father does for his children. For who has ever heard of a child who never had to be corrected? (TPT)

Chapter 15

1. John 10:10 The thief cometh not, but for to steal, and to kill, and to destroy: I am come that they might have life, and that they might have it more abundantly.

2. Galatians 3:29 And if ye be Christ's, then are ye Abraham's seed, and heirs according to the promise.

3. Strongs's Concordance-Strong's Number 1680-elpis

4. Strongs's Concordance-Strong's Number 308- anablepo

5. Romans 11:29 For the gifts and calling of God are without repentance.

About the Author

Randall Rittenberry lives in Cookeville, Tennessee with his wife, Cynthia. He has two children, Seth and his wife Jacklyn, and Victoria and her husband, Matt. He also has four grandchildren, Madilynn and Michael, Viviana and Ezra. Since 1995, he has served as a counselor, pastor, and teacher. He has served in, and developed, ministries within the local church including: helps (ushers and greeters), children's ministry, youth ministry, and worship. He has held leadership and administrative positions in churches, including being an associate pastor and senior pastor, and also a national ministerial organization. Randall holds a degree in theology from Impact Int'l School of Ministry. He has a passion to help people develop to their full potential, become disciples of Jesus, and to see themselves the way God sees them. For more info go to:

www.randallrittenberry.com

You can find teaching resources there such as videos, podcasts, and articles. You can also find him on YouTube.

Other books by this author:

Discovering Purpose
Finding God's Plan For Your Life

Psalm 19:14 Setting Your Heart
Scriptures To Renew Your Mind and
Establish Your Heart

These can be found on Amazon or at the author's website:
www.randallrittenberry.com